# MEDITATIONS OF THE HEART

*Let the words of my mouth, and the meditation of my heart, be acceptable in thy sight, O Lord, my strength, and my redeemer.*

*PSALM 19:14*

# MEDITATIONS
## of
# THE HEART

by

HOWARD THURMAN

RICHMOND
INDIANA

Library of Congress Cataloging in Publication Data

Thurman, Howard, 1900-1981
  Meditations of the heart.

  Reprint of the 1953 ed. published by Harper & Row, New York.
  1. Devotional literature. I. Title.
(BV4832.2.T55 1976)      242      76-18287
ISBN 0-913408-25-5

To

ELEANOR LLOYD SMITH

in whom the inner and the outer are one

**Editor's note:**

We realize that inclusive language is noticeably absent in Howard Thurman's writings. As gifted and prophetic as he was, Howard Thurman was also a product of his times, and inclusive language was not a part of the social consciousness.

Regardless of language, the substance of Howard Thurman's work is inclusive. His life and theology were inclusive, and if he were writing today his language would more accurately reflect this worldview.

# CONTENTS

## II. THE BINDING TIES

## III. LIFE IS ALIVE

# FOREWORD

This is volume two of *Deep is the Hunger*. These meditations were written originally for use by me and the congregation of "Fellowship Church." Some of them were used as meditation "working papers" in the Quiet Time from ten-thirty to eleven o'clock on Sunday morning. Others appeared on the back of the calendar for the regular weekly worship service. Each meditation comes out of what is essentially a laboratory situation. Their use has already been tested.

Due to the circumstances which brought them forth, there is no unifying theme by which they are held together. They are addressed to some of the deep and insistent needs of the human spirit, which needs know no age, clime, culture or group. They are needs that are universal and in which all men share. Their purpose is to focus the mind and the heart upon God as the Eternal Source and Goal of life. Wherever they seem stumbling, weak and stammering, understand that they are the utterances of one who sees through "a glass darkly." Whatever light they may bring at any point in another's darkness is but a glimmer of "the Light that lighteth every man that cometh into the world."

My personal thanks are extended to all who have shared in any way in making this volume possible. Special appreciation goes to Miss Grace Marrett who studied the entire manuscript and, in addition to thoughtful suggestions, prepared the table of contents to make the book of more practical use to the reader; to Mrs. J. Stewart Burgess who helped in the earlier classification of material; to Mrs. Joseph Williams who typed the first copy; to Mrs. Alyce Walker, editor of the *Growing Edge*, for many helpful aids, and to my secretary, Mrs. Alice Ratner, without whose patience the necessary work on this volume would not have been done.

# I

## *The Inward Sea*

1here is in every person an inward sea, and in that sea there is an island and on that island there is an altar and standing guard before that altar is the "angel with the flaming sword." Nothing can get by that angel to be placed upon that altar unless it has the mark of your inner authority. Nothing passes "the angel with the flaming sword" to be placed upon your altar unless it be a part of "the fluid area of your consent." This is your crucial link with the Eternal.

# 1. An Island of Peace within One's Soul

A BEAUTIFUL and significant phrase, "Island of Peace within one's own soul." The individual lives his life in the midst of a wide variety of stresses and strains. There are many tasks in which he is engaged that are not meaningful to him even though they are important in secondary ways. There are many responsibilities that are his by virtue of training, or family, or position. Again and again, decisions must be made as to small and large matters; each one involves him in devious ways. No one is ever free from the peculiar pressures of his own life. Each one has to deal with the evil aspects of life, with injustices inflicted upon him and injustices which he wittingly or unwittingly inflicts upon others. We are all of us deeply involved in the throes of our own weaknesses and strengths, expressed often in the profoundest conflicts within our own souls. The only hope for surcease, the only possibility of stability for the person, is to establish an Island of Peace within one's own soul. Here one brings for review the purposes and dreams to which one's life is tied. This is the place where there is no pretense, no dishonesty, no adulteration. What passes over the threshold is simon-pure. What one really thinks and feels about one's own life stands revealed; what one really thinks and feels about other people far and near is seen with every nuance honestly labeled: love is love, hate is hate, fear is fear. Well within the island is the Temple where God dwells—not the God of the creed, the church, the family, but the God of one's heart. Into His Presence one comes with all of one's problems and faces His scrutiny. What a man is, what his plans are, what his authentic point is, where his life goes—all is available to him in the Presence. How foolish it is, how terrible, if you have not found your Island of Peace within your own soul! It means that you are living without the discovery of your true home.

## 2. Silence is a Door to God

THERE is very great virtue in the cultivation of silence, and strength to be found in using it as a door to God. Such a door opens within. When I have quieted down, I must spend some time in self-examination in the Presence of God. This is no facile admission of guilt for wrongs done or a too quick labeling of attitudes in negative terms. But it does mean lifting up a part of one's self and turning it over and over, viewing it from many angles and then holding it still as one waits for the movement of God's spirit in judgment, in honesty and in understanding. To examine one's self in introspection and inner probing may become sheer morbidity, but to examine one's self in the climate and the mood of prayer, carries with it a kind of lift and positiveness that is at once the antidote to morbidity. Every period of prayer should provide for an experience of self-examination in the presence of God. Self-examination issues most often in a sense of sin, the acknowledgment of which is the first step in the forgiveness of God. It is at such a moment that a man sees that the wrongdoing of which he may be guilty is a wrongdoing against God. "Against Thee and Thee only have I sinned and done this evil in Thy sight." Such is always the final testimony of the spirit in self-examination in the Presence of God. There may be, very directly following this phase of prayer, a time of thanksgiving. Thanksgiving in the Presence of God becomes more than perfunctory. Thanksgiving has implicit within the idea itself a sensitive appraisal. Suddenly, I may become aware that that which I thought was the sheer result of my own effort came my way despite my effort. In the Presence of God, His radiance picks up the magic in so much that I had taken for granted. Somehow in thanksgiving I see clearly, if but for a fleeting moment, that much, much has come my way as a normal part of my dependency, without my being aware of it. It is at such moments that I may become literally overwhelmed by a profound sense of the love and the grace of God. The very roots of my own pride lie exposed to the scrutiny of God, and if I can bear it over and over again, the very will to pride of that kind may be destroyed in me; yes, destroyed by the sheer love of God. Perhaps, it is always true that the test of my thanksgiving is the humility which it inspires. Self-examination—thanksgiving—humility—let us experience them in our quiet time in the presence of God.

### 3. In Quiet One Discovers the Will of God

IN THE quiet time I may seek to discover the will of God
for my own life. This quest must be pursued with great
diligence and consecutiveness. It is well to use a part of each
period in seeking to find the answer or, more important, clues
to the answer, to this deeply felt need. A man wants to know
that his life's purposes and plans are floored by a structure
that is more than he is, that is comprehensive, significant
and good. When there is the assurance that such a structure
has been found, then the sense of being adrift, of living a
meaningless life, disappears. The simple assumption is, that
God is in each one of us, a part of our very life structure,
and we are in Him. We need not concern ourselves over-
much with the many speculative questions that may range
through our minds as a result of such assumption. For the
assumption is in itself something more; it is an insistent fact,
a category which is the rock upon which we stand. It is its
own evidence. Very important indeed is it to be aware of
the direction which begins to take shape within us as we seek
to know the Will with all our hearts. Often, the will of God
becomes apparent in the central concern of our spirits,
which leads us to act or function in accordance with its
urgency. Or it may become clear to us only after we have
exhausted all our plans and schemes for doing certain things
or achieving certain results with our lives. Sometimes a man
goes along very sure of his direction and then, under the

scrutiny of a deadly serious searching in the experience of prayer, finds that all along he has been mistaken. Often, only one step at the time becomes clear, while for some others, in a flash of insight, the total meaning of their lives is made clear. God is a part of the very content of one's own life. Sometimes, His will is seen in simple earnestness and intense desire. Sometimes the quieting of one's spirit in prayer exposes the area of sensitiveness to God's spirit which is submerged by much traffic. Sometimes, there is the marshaling of one's ideas, plans and purposes in accordance with the sense of direction which looms larger and larger as the *must* for one's life. Always there is the checking and rechecking, testing and retesting, of one's life in the light of what seems more and more the right course, the right way for one's life. At length one's entire life—no particular aspect of it but one's entire life—becomes pervaded with a quality which is the divine quality, an accent which is the divine accent.

## 4. Relief in Voicing One's Feelings

O Lord, how long shall I cry for help, and thou wilt not hear, cry to thee "Violence" and thou *wilt* not save?

THE prayer experience must ever take into account the times of dryness, of denials, of emptiness. The reasons for this are numerous. It may be due to scattered thoughts or attachment to plans, ideas or experiences that break the divine accord; or to bad timing, when the mood of prayer is strangely alien to the spirit; or to the movement of the spirit of God in a manner unpredictable and strange. It is very instructive that the mystics, despite their insistence upon the necessity of spiritual disciplines or exercises, are careful to point out that the exercises themselves do not guarantee the "coming of the spirit" or an awareness of the Presence. Always undergirding prayer there must be an attitude of trust and confidence that submits one's total enterprise to the Will and the Mind of God. But sometimes the urgency is so great, the pain growing out of the need so overwhelming, that the anguish and frustration spill over into a cry which in itself becomes a judgment and a startling accusation! "How long shall I cry for help, and thou wilt not hear? . . . I cry to thee 'Violence.' " Often there is great relief in being able to put into words the quality or the very nuance of need and suffering. To suffer in dumb silence, to be able to find no word capable of voicing what is being experienced, seems degrading to the self because it pushes the individual back into a vast feeling continuum from which he has emerged into a personality, self-conscious and self-aware. Man was a *feeling* creature long before he was a *thinking* creature. The mind is younger than the body and younger than the emotions. When we are articulate, it means that detachment from immediate experience makes possible an ability to name it. This seems to characterize the divine act always. When the individual is thus able to voice his profoundest feelings, he sees himself, quite unconsciously, presenting God with a compulsion on his behalf. There is added challenge in the words if they *name* what is happening.

### 5. The God of Life is the God of Religion

Why dost thou make me see wrongs
    and look upon trouble?
Destruction and violence are before me;
    strife and contention arise.

THE idea that God is responsible for ills in life is a great safety valve for the spirit of man. And yet it is much more. It springs out of a deeper insight: ultimately there must be no distinction between the God of Life and the God of Religion. All events in life take place, somehow, within the divine context. The tendency to fix responsibility is inescapable. If responsibility for ills can be pinned down, then the possibility of attacking and uprooting them is very real. This possibility is in the profound confidence that a structure of moral integrity undergirds all of life; that such a structure is basic in the totality of all experience. Things do not happen, merely; they are a part of some kind of rationale. If this can be tracked down and understood, then the living experience, however terrible, makes sense. Even though one is never able to accomplish this tracking down, one cannot destroy the confidence that the logic of all ills is knowable. A man traces them as far as he can, until, at last, he seeks no longer to understand the ills but rather to *understand* God's *understanding*. Lacking this, he rests himself in the assurance of God's Presence in him and in life about him. He sees the travail of his own soul and is satisfied.

## 6. "Be Still and Cool in the Mind"

IN THE diary of George Fox there appears this very significant sentence: "Be still and cool in thy own mind and spirit,
from thy own thoughts, and then thou wilt feel the principle
of God to turn thy mind to the Lord from whence cometh
life; whereby thou mayest receive the strength and power
to allay all storms and tempests." This is an important result
of the habitual use of the quietness that a man can carry
around inside of him. It is a central stillness of spirit that
is so vital that it can tame the wildness out of almost any
tempest, however raging it may be. Of course the individual
must desire this to happen. Sometimes there are ragings of
anxiety, of hurts that we do not want to see disappear. They
provide excellent opportunities to bolster up our own ego
or own sense of faltering security. This fact must not blind
us to the great power that there is in what is here referred
to as the central stillness. For it is in the quiet which invades
us and which becomes a characteristic of our total respiration
that we are most acutely aware of the operation of the
 Presence of God. Here is the "mercy seat" of God before
which all things are stripped to their true essence and their
real character revealed. The plans and purposes of our times,
the primary and secondary levels of our desiring, the fateful
issues of our loves and hates, the ground of our own faith
are established and confirmed. There is a wonderful lift to the
spirit in knowing that the way is always channeled so that
it may have free access to the mind and the cleansing power

of God. "Be still and cool in thy own mind and spirit, from thy own thoughts, and then thou wilt feel the principle of God to turn thy mind to the Lord from whence cometh life."

## 7. The Pattern of Prayer

EVEN the most cursory examination of the prayer habit which has developed within the Christian tradition, reveals the fact that a certain basic structure is quite evident. The structure is very simple and very sound. First, there is a recollection of God expressed in various ways: the form of address—Our Father, or Holy Father, God of our Fathers, O Lord; there may be other words of recognition or greeting or salutation expressing a feeling of closeness, fellowship, sometimes even fear and dependence. There is usually involved in this *naming*, words which recall to the mind God's relation to His world—He is Creator, Giver of Life, Sustainer of Life, Redeemer, Judge, Righteous Will, Friend, Companion. A recognition of God brings with it a feeling and a thought of one's attitude toward One who is regarded as Creator or Redeemer. This mood is most naturally expressed in some form of thanksgiving and praise. It is important to say that such a feeling is most natural—it is not to suggest merely that God requires it. The mood of thanksgiving inspires an awareness of individual shortcomings and failures expressing themselves in contrition, confession and a deep desire for forgiveness. Forgiveness nets a sense of being cleansed, purified, which cleansing and purification must be spelled out in the fabric of one's living by the changes in behavior which undergird the sense of cleansing. There follows quite normally the sharing of one's personal desires, hopes and needs with One who understands. These longings are usually cast in the form of personal petitions of one kind or another. What enters here comes under the scrutiny of God, and often many changes, even in their form, take place. From this step, it is simple to move to the sharing of one's desires and hopes for others, and one's sense of need which the whole human family shares—the need for peace, for health, for justice and for decency. Once these are deeply shared with God, it becomes clear at what points one must share with God in the whole task of redeeming human life. It is never quite sufficient to place all the needs of mankind before God and leave them there. The efficacy of the prayer is often measured by the degree to which the individual is willing to become involved in actually working in the world to meet these needs. A man may share in his prayer his concern for peace in the world and yet, in his own little world, be unwilling to change his private attitude of antagonism or prejudice toward his fellows. Obviously, such prayer would be meaningless. Of course, this pattern of prayer that has evolved does not take into account those spontaneous outpourings of the heart and mind to God. Prayer at its best is revealed when a man enjoys God and prays out of sheer love of Him.

## 8. A Lull in the Rhythm of Doing

THE place of prayer and meditation in the life of modern man is limited and hedged in by the multiplicity of details to which attention must be given as a normal part of daily experience. It is true that in some sense a man's whole life may be regarded as his prayer. Ordinarily, what a man does is an expression of his intent, and his intent is the focusing of his desiring, and his desires are the prayers of his heart. But such explanations are far from satisfactory. There is no argument needed for the necessity of taking time out for being alone, for withdrawal, for being quiet without and still within. The sheer physical necessity is urgent because the body and the entire nervous system cry out for the healing waters of silence. One could not begin the cultivation of the prayer life at a more practical point than deliberately to seek each day, and several times a day, a lull in the rhythm of daily doing, a period when nothing happens that demands active participation. It is a wonderful way with which to begin the day and to bring one's day to an end. At first the quiet times may be quite barren or merely a retreat from exhaustion. One has to get used to the stillness even after it has been achieved. The time may be used for taking stock, for examining one's life direction, one's plans, one's relations, and the like. This in itself is most profitable. It is like cleaning out the closets, or the desk drawers, and getting things in order. The time may be used for focusing and re-focusing one's purposes in the light of what at first may be only one's

idea of the best and the highest. Then quiet changes begin
to take place. Somewhere along the way, one's idea of the
best and the highest takes on a transcendent character and one
begins to commune, to communicate with one's idea of the
best and the highest—only a man does not talk to, or with,
an idea. When the awareness of God comes in—how He
entered, one does not know—one is certain that He has been
there all the time. This assurance is categorical and becomes
the very core of one's faith; indeed, it becomes more and
more one's faith. Suppose you begin now, this day, with the
use of the quiet time in some such fashion as suggested.

## 9. How Good to Center Down!

How good it is to center down!
To sit quietly and see one's self pass by!
The streets of our minds seethe with endless traffic;
Our spirits resound with clashings, with noisy silences,
While something deep within hungers and thirsts for the still
    moment and the resting lull.
With full intensity we seek, ere the quiet passes, a fresh sense
    of order in our living;
A direction, a strong sure purpose that will structure our con-
    fusion and bring meaning in our chaos.
We look at ourselves in this waiting moment—the kinds of
    people we are.
The questions persist: what are we doing with our lives?—
    what are the motives that order our days?

What is the end of our doings? Where are we trying to go?
Where do we put the emphasis and where are our values
     focused?
For what end do we make sacrifices? Where is my treasure
     and what do I love most in life?
What do I hate most in life and to what am I true?
Over and over the questions beat in upon the waiting moment.
As we listen, floating up through all the jangling echoes of
     our turbulence, there is a sound of another kind—
A deeper note which only the stillness of the heart makes
     clear.
It moves directly to the core of our being. Our questions are
     answered,
Our spirits refreshed, and we move back into the traffic of
     our daily round
With the peace of the Eternal in our step.
How good it is to center down!

## 10. In the Moment of Pause, the Vision of God

IT IS good to make an end of movement, to come to a point
of rest, a place of pause. There is some strange magic in
activity, in keeping at it, in continuing to be involved in
many things that excite the mind and keep the hours swiftly
passing. But it is a deadly magic; one is not wise to trust it
with too much confidence.

The moment of pause, the point of rest, has its own magic.
A man comes to such a moment with all the confusion of his

life full upon him. At first only a tiny fragment of himself
is he able to bring into his moment of pause. Often the only
thing he is able to muster is the great and overwhelming
need for a little haven of rest for his churning and deeply
involved spirit. The moment comes sometimes after definite
preparation. When that happens, there is a sense of being
ready, of having one's house in order for the receiving of
the Guest. The preparations vary in accordance with the
temper of the persons and the gravity of the need. Certainly
a part of the preparation is a quiet place—where possible, a
physical surrounding that does not fight against the mood.
There should not be too great physical weariness. If there is
no alternative, then the time of pause becomes a time of
sheer physical renewal. This is not to be despised, but it is
also not to be confused with a movement of a deeper level
of one's life.

Often there is a real struggle to call in one's self from some
phase of experience that has one deeply involved in a con-
suming fashion. It is often quite subtle. The experience keeps
claiming one's thoughts, one's unconscious attention. The
hold may be so great upon the life that one has to tear away
literally, leaving a part bleeding and lacerated, as mute but
dramatic testimony to the searching character of one's in-
volvement. There is an inner insistence toward wholeness and
it is this that the moment, the experience of quiet, announces.
It is a fearful announcement: "BRING IN YOUR SCATTERED
PARTS, BE PRESENT AT ALL THE LEVELS OF YOUR CONSCIOUS-
NESS. THIS IS THE TIME OF TOGETHERNESS. ONLY HE WHO

HAS COME TO A POINT OF HOLY FOCUS, MAY BE BLESSED WITH THE VISION OF GOD."

And without the vision of God, there can at last be no significance in living.

## 11. We Lay Bare all that We Are

OUR Father, we turn to Thee in the quietness of this meditation period. It is but natural that we expose to Thee the things in us that seem most worthy and good that we may delight Thy Spirit and joy Thy Heart. The unworthy and the ugly things in us we almost instinctively seek to hide, to cover up, that we may seem pleasing in Thy Sight. But deep within us we know that this is not enough. We know that somehow we must be totally exposed to Thee, holding back nothing, seeking refuge behind no protecting screen or darkening shadows. We do not keep back the unsightly from Thee because we cannot trust Thee, dare not run the risk, but because we cannot deny the urge to offer in prayer the best that is in us.

Teach us to know that Thy love is so whole and so healing that nothing less than all of us can rise to meet Thine all-encompassing care. Teach us to share with Thee the good and the bad in us, the ugly and the beautiful, the clean and the sordid, the success and the failure—all, everything complete in every part. With penitence for fumblings, failures, ignorances and sins; with thanksgiving for directness, suc-

cesses, knowledge and rightness, we lay bare all that we are
to Thy love and Thy understanding, O God our Father.

## 12. Work and Rest are one Entity

RUYSBROECK writes, "God comes to us without ceasing . . .
and demands of us both action and fruition, in such a way
that one never impedes but always strengthens the other. And
therefore the most inward man lives his life in these two
ways: namely, in work and in rest. And in each he is whole
and undivided; for he is wholly in God because he rests in
fruition, and he is wholly in himself because he loves in
activity; and he is perpetually called and urged by God to
renew both the rest and the work." We are accustomed to
recognizing the interplay between work and rest in making
for healthy living. This is expressed in many ways. We know
that we cannot keep our bodies going if we do not refuel by
eating and by sleeping. Over and over again, we provide for
a change of pace in our life routine to the end that we shall
not burn out or rust out. A commonplace adage that expresses
one facet of the problem is: "All work and no play makes
Jack a dull boy." A music score that provides for no rests,
no devaluation of whole notes, would be unbearable at long
last. Here we are face to face with a life principle. One man
has designated it as a principle of alternation. Even casual
reflection would lead one to recognize that a very urgent
function of the quiet time is to provide a breather for the
spirit, opportunity for catching up, reorganizing and re-eval-

uating the endless activities in which we are involved daily and hourly. Ruysbroeck very wisely makes of both work and rest one entity, one single unit. Further, he recognizes each as being a part of the demand of God for our lives. How curious it is that we should think of religious life as confined to activity, to getting things done! Of course this is an important and crucial part of the religious imperative. But there is more. Careful provision must be made for rest, for quiet, for prayer and for renewal. This, not as something other than activity and function, but rather as that which is an integral part of the religious life itself. When we function, we are enjoined to function *wholly*, bringing into the deeds the wisdom and the insight of the quiet and the pause. When we rest we are enjoined to rest *wholly*, bringing into the quiet time the sense of doing and participating in the activities that claim our energies. "The most inward man lives his life in these two ways: namely, in work and in rest."

## 13. None Need Be Alone

FOR some there awaits along the way always the vision bright to cheer the path and lift the load aloft. The glory of the shining light surrounds the simplest deed, the hardest choice, the heaviest care. Theirs is not the lot to be in doubt, to wander lost amidst the shadows of their hills. They know not how it comes, nor whence; they only know the look expectant and the grand surmise.

There are some who know the vision and its fearful cost in deep despair and rugged quest. There are no forerunners of the light to come, no stirring of the inward parts to alert the heart and calm the mind. Wrestling, struggling, searching, seeking; for them this is the only way by which surcease is found. Sometimes a sharp resentment of their *fact* darts along the channels of the mind, tearing the tender tendrils of their hopes in bitter threads. Aghast, they watch the question form: Why must it always be like this for me?

There are some to whom the vision never comes and long ago they learned that such is not their way. For them the road is never rough, nor smooth; the light is never bright, nor does it quite go out. The long silent path reveals no sudden turns, no glad surprise. Anchored to a sure monotony, they gather just strength sufficient for the daily need—no more, no less. They only see with little eyes, they seem supported by little strengths, they move along with little hopes.

"Father, to each of Thy children according to his need, pour out the riches of Thy grace that none need be alone and none may seek another's light . . . Amen."

## 14. Two Kinds of Ideals

Two kinds of ideals are always at work in the lives of men. There are those ideals that are ultimate and in a very real sense always far out beyond anything that can be achieved. Or as one person puts it, they are like far-off lighthouses whose glow is far away in the distance. They belong to the realm of the absolute and are never marred by the sordidness of the surroundings in which men work and struggle. They are perfect in all their structure and the vision of them quickens the pulse and kindles the desire for the real, but the unattainable. They are very important in the life of the race because they keep alive a perennial hope that the best may yet sometime come to be in fact what it is in fancy. Life would be very poor and wretched without them. What creates them is ever a mystery; they belong to life and yet they are something other than life.

There are also those ideals that seem to be created out of the stubborn realities, in the midst of which men work and live. They belong essentially to the stuff of life, the very raw materials of experience. They are never separate from what a man knows to be the character of his daily living. Always they are close at hand, a part of the immediate possibility, always being achieved but never quite fully achieved. With reference to these latter ideals a man is never disillusioned, he knows deep within himself that they belong to his world, to his striving. Always they seem to float just above the ebb and flow of all his moments. Their chief characteristic is that they belong. As long as a man is alive, though he may fail again and again, he is sure they are a part of all his striving.

It is well within the range of possibility that these two kinds of ideals will in time prove to be of one piece. The present ever-achieving ideal is seen as the nearer end of the far-reaching and ultimate ideal. When this happens, a man experiences the integration of his life. He becomes deeply assured that what he is striving for in his little world is suddenly a part of the larger whole. He is no longer alone in his striving. If he be religious, what he strives for at his best, what he seeks where he is, when he is most himself, is what God is seeking in the great ends that guide ultimately the destiny of all of life. Such a man finds a place which is uniquely his place and most naturally seeks the strength of God to stabilize him in his most commonplace striving.

## 15. Keep Alive the Dream in the Heart

As LONG as a man has a dream in his heart, he cannot lose the significance of living. It is a part of the pretensions of modern life to traffic in what is generally called "realism." There is much insistence upon being practical, down to earth. Such things as dreams are wont to be regarded as romantic or as a badge of immaturity, or as escape hatches for the human spirit. When such a mood or attitude is carefully scrutinized, it is found to be made up largely of pretensions, in short, of bluff. Men cannot continue long to live if the dream in the heart has perished. It is then that they stop hoping, stop looking, and the last embers of their anticipations fade away.

The dream in the heart is the outlet. It is one with the living water welling up from the very springs of Being, nourishing and sustaining all of life. Where there is no dream, the life becomes a swamp, a dreary dead place and, deep within, a man's heart begins to rot. The dream need not be some great and overwhelming plan; it need not be a dramatic picture of what might or must be someday; it need not be a concrete outpouring of a world-shaking possibility of sure fulfillment. Such may be important for some; such may be crucial for a particular moment of human history. But it is not in these grand ways that the dream nourishes life. The dream is the quiet persistence in the heart that enables a man to ride out the storms of his churning experiences. It is the exciting whisper moving through the aisles of his spirit answering the monotony of limitless days of dull routine. It is the ever-recurring melody in the midst of the broken harmony and harsh discords of human conflict. It is the touch of significance which highlights the ordinary experience, the common event. The dream is no outward thing. It does not take its rise from the environment in which one moves or functions. It lives in the inward parts, it is deep within, where the issues of life and death are ultimately determined. Keep alive the dream; for as long as a man has a dream in his heart, he cannot lose the significance of living.

## 16. Judgment Belongs to God

IT IS a very subtle temptation to decide that the negative deeds which flow from one's life to others are not expressive of one's real intent. There seems ever available some extra or extenuating circumstance that gives a ready alibi for such deeds. How easily the excuses come: "I have had a very bad day," or "For some reason I got up on the wrong side of the bed," or "I have met with so many personàl reverses recently that . . ." or "I have always had a quick temper; it is just one of those things . . ." Always there is a ready supply of excuses for the negative deed. Very rarely is one willing to face the fact, even when it is true, that the negative deed was what was really intended.

But when the picture shifts! The negative deed that comes from others to me is apt to be regarded by me as deliberate. It is very difficult for us to entertain any notion other than that it was intended. How often are we tempted to say or to think, "He pretends to be so courteous and gracious but this kind of thing shows his true colors," or "I cannot understand how a self-respecting human being could do such a thing; but one never knows . . ." What we allow ourselves we only grudgingly admit for others.

There are two suggestions, simple but far-reaching. One is, that it is well to be mindful that so much which is negative has moved from one's self toward others that it is sound to practice charity toward others for the negative things that move from others toward one's self. This means the relaxing of the will to ascribe to others motives that one denies when the same motives are ascribed to one's self. The other suggestion is, that in the final analysis, judgment belongs to God. Every judgment that I pass upon my fellows is a self-judgment. Judgment can only be whole and creative when it takes place in a context of full and absolute knowledge. Full and absolute knowledge even of one's self is never possible; how can it be with reference to others? Again, it becomes us to say with true humility, "Judgment belongs to God"; and one can only pray, "Search me, O God, and know my heart!"

## 17. That Thy Tryst may be Kept

For a long time I thought that the saints, the mystics, the individuals deeply concerned about religion regarded spiritual exercises as prerequisites for the inflooding of the living God. These prerequisites seemed to be regarded as the disciplines, the faithful carrying out of which would bring the Presence of God actively into awareness. And yet I have often found that the sense of the Presence of God may not always be experienced in prayer and in meditation. The disciplines may be fulfilled and yet the life remain unillumined. Then there are other times when one has the sense of being invaded by the Spirit of God even though one is not involved in any of the disciplines.

Upon further reflection, it would seem that an important function of the exercises is to build an immunity against the confusion and the distractions of environment. They seem to make a clearing in the woods in which one may be still. They provide the technique for disentangling the mind and spirit from their involvements, that the tryst may be kept with the Spirit. They do not guarantee that the Spirit will be encountered but they do prepare the way of response to its movement.

"Take the dimness of my soul away"—this seems to be the

central function of spiritual exercises. This is enough!
Enough!


### 18. Every Judgment is Self-judgment

IT IS very easy to sit in judgment upon the behavior of others
but often difficult to realize that every judgment is a self-
judgment. A corollary to this fact is the finding again and
again that the thing which seems to me objectionable in others
is something of which I myself am guilty. Queer, isn't it?
For a few weeks, during a summer series on a university
campus, I shared a suite with two other men. The suite con-
sisted of two bedrooms, a bath and a living room. The two
men occupied one of the bedrooms and I, the other. One
night when I came in, as I opened the door, I heard a voice
say, "Pipe down, for Pete's sake, pipe down." This was followed by the soft thud of a pillow being thrown against the
wall. In a few minutes one of the fellows stood at the door
with disheveled hair and distraught features. "I can't go to
sleep. Have you ever heard such snoring? Usually I get off
first and then his snoring does not disturb me but tonight
he went to bed early. There ought to be a law against it. Why
doesn't his wife tell him, or maybe she is a snorer herself.
What a partner to a snoring duet he would make!" I replied
that there was an extra bed in my room which he could share
if my reading lamp would not keep him awake. He accepted
gladly, assuring me that the light would not disturb him.
After he had retired and I had settled down for an hour's

reading, I became aware of his heavy breathing. Then it began—the most pronounced and heavy snoring that I had ever heard in my life. Finally, I could not continue my reading and I knew that sleep would be impossible. I went into the living room, where I spent the night on the couch. I had meant to awaken early, before he did, so as not to embarrass him. But I overslept. When he saw me he said, "Oh no! Don't tell me. I'll never blow my top again about snorers." The only creative attitude toward the weaknesses or the disabilities of others is a quiet humility. What I condemn in others may be but a reflection of myself in a mirror.

## 19. A Man Becomes his Dream

IT IS always miraculous to see a dream take shape and form. Dreams in themselves are made of the chiffon of men's hopes, desires and aspirings. There may be no limit to their fabulous unfolding, rich in all the magic of the fantastic. A dream may be held at the focal point of one's mind and heart until it takes over the total process of one's thinking and planning, until at last a man becomes the living embodiment of what he dreams. This is the first miracle: a man becomes his dream; then it is that the line between what he does and is and his dream melts away. A new accent appears in how he thinks, the signature of his dream must guarantee the integrity of his every act. In some ways he seems to be one possessed; and perhaps this is true. The second miracle appears when the outline of the dream begins to take objective shape, when it begins to become concrete and to take its place among the particular facts of life. This means that something more than the man becomes the embodiment of the dream. Others begin to see the manifestation and to feel the pull of its challenge. In turn, through sheer contagion, they relate themselves to it and its demands. If the embodiment takes the form of an institution it means that at the center of the institution there is a living, pulsing core which guarantees not only flexibility but also a continuous unfolding in an increasing dimension of creativity. Hence, men who have become embodiments of a dream, project an institution which becomes the embodiment of the dream which they themselves have already embodied. It is of the very nature of such a dream that it continues to grow, to develop, to find ever more creative dimensions. Hence the dream is always receding; it can never be contained in a life, however perfect. So it is with the institution which is its embodiment. It must always maintain its dynamic character, and its greatest significance must ever be found in the new heights to which it calls all who share its contagion.

## 20. Memories Crowd upon Us

MEMORIES crowd upon us as we look back over the week just passed:

Many high hopes—many dreams unfulfilled;
Many blunders made and, in the sharpness of our anguish,
We would turn back the wheels of time and try again.

Many joys that were unanticipated;
Many little graces by which our faith in ourselves and in life
Is lifted up and strengthened—
Much for which we need to be forgiven;
Much we need to forgive.

All around us, our Father, there are reminders of Thy Pres-
ence in our midst:
Pangs of conscience,
A spontaneous impulse to do the kind and gracious thing,
The sensitiveness to another's needs,
The great burden of anguish which we feel as we look out
upon the world.

Teach us, O living Spirit, the wisdom to lay ourselves
Bare to Thy scrutiny—that we may reflect Thy life
In the dark places of our minds, hearts and desires;
That we may know Thy courage—and the grounds of Thy
hope
For the children of men.

## 21. The Great Exposure

SOMETIMES there is only a sixty-second divide between youth
and maturity, childhood and adulthood, strength and weakness, life and death. That life is vulnerable is the key to its
longevity. We are surrounded every day by the exposure to
sudden and devastating calamity. Despite all efforts to the

contrary, there is no device by which we may get immunity from the "slings and arrows of outrageous fortune." Here is a man in the full prime of active life, with all the strength and vigor of a rounded maturity—disease strikes, he withers and dies quickly, without warning and often without pre-monition. Here is a carefree happy child surrounded by all the love that wise devotion and careless rapture can give—a plane crash, both parents perish and what at ten o'clock was a child becomes, at ten-one, a desolate creature shunted across the Great Divide that separates hope from hopelessness, dependence from independence. Thus it goes in one vein.

Or here is a person for whom all the lights had long since gone out, the way ahead is no way—a sharp, sudden turn in the road or a chance encounter in the darkness and everything is changed. Life is vulnerable—always there is the exposed flank.

Sometimes much energy is spent in a vain attempt to pro-tect one's self. We try to harden our fiber, to render ourselves safe from exposure. We refuse to love anyone because we cannot risk being hurt. We withdraw from participation in the struggles of our fellows because we must not get caught in the communal agony of those around us. We take no stand where fateful issues are at stake because we dare not run the risk of exposure to attack. But all this, at long last, is of no avail. The attack from without is missed and we escape only to find that the life we have protected has slowly and quietly sickened deep within because it was cut off from the nourish-ment of the Great Exposure. It is the way of life that it be nourished and sustained by the constant threat, the sudden rending.

Then

> Welcome each rebuff
> That makes life's smoothness, rough

## 22. Life, an Offering to God

MANY, many years ago, a Hindu poet wrote:

> Love not the world nor yet forsake
> Its gifts in fear and hate.
> Thy life to God an offering make,
> And to Him dedicate.

We are all of us involved in life in its varied aspects and responsibilities. The daily routine carries its own toll of energies and processes. The struggle for bread and shelter continues to the very end to beat at our lives and our very spirits with an insistence that cannot be ignored. For many there are additional cares that go beyond the demands of our own personal survival and encompass the tender threads of the lives of others to whom we are bound by ties of blood and birth. Beyond all this, there are areas of the common life in which we must do our part in order that the very fabric of society may be maintained against collapse and disintegration. There are dreams, hopes and yearnings which possess our lives, calling us away from the usual round and the common tasks. In the midst of all these pressures and many more,

life for us becomes entangled or again and again bogs down.
There comes a moment when we are in utter revolt—something deep within us becomes tired, weary, exhausted and
finally, outraged. What we long for in deep anxiety is some
haven, some place of retreat, some time of quiet where our
bruised and shredded spirits may find healing and restoration.
One form that this anxiety takes is to hate life and to fear
tomorrow. For such the ancient poet speaks a timely word.
All such experiences are a part of our experience and must
be regarded as life's gifts. Whatever may be the uniqueness
of a man's experience, he must remember that nothing that
is happening to him is separated from that which is common
to man. The answer to all of this reaction of deep anxiety
and anguish is, says the poet: "Thy life to God an offering
make, and to Him dedicate." And the meaning of this? If I
make of my life an offering and a dedication to God, then
this dedication will include all of my entanglements and
involvements. There follows, then, a radical change over my
entire landscape and miraculously I am free at my center. It
is for this reason that it is well, again and again, to re-estab-
lish my dedication, to make repeatedly an offering of my life.
I must keep my dedication up to date with my experiencing.

## 23. Thou Shalt Love

THOU shalt love thy God. There must be for me a deep sense
of relatedness to God. This relatedness is the way by which
there shall open for me more and more springs of energy

and power, which will enable me to thread life's mysteries with life's clue. It is this, and this alone, that will make it possible for me to stand anything that life can or may do to me. I shall not waste any effort in trying to reduce God to my particular logic. Here in the quietness, I shall give myself in love to God.

Thou shalt love thy neighbor. How I must seek ever the maintenance of the kind of relatedness to others that will feed the springs of kindness and sympathy in me! I shall study how I may be tender without being soft; gracious without being ingratiating; kind without being sentimental; and understanding without being judgmental. Here in the quietness, I shall give myself in love to my neighbors.

Thou shalt love Thyself. I must learn to love myself with detachment. I must have no attitude toward myself that contributes to my own delinquency. I shall study how so to love myself that, in my attitude toward myself, I shall be pleasing to God and face with confidence what He requires of me. Here in the quietness, I give myself over to the kind of self-regard that would make me whole and clean in my own sight and in the sight of God.

> Thou shalt love
> Thy God
> Thy neighbor
> Thyself

## 24. God is With Me

*Thou art with me.*

*God is with me,* in the sense that He is the Creator and the Sustainer of life. This is a part of my general thought and experience. There is something so big and vast about God as Creator and Sustainer of all of life that it is hard for me to feel that I am included.

*God is with me.* All around me are certain expressions of orderliness, of beauty, of wonder and delight. The regularity of sunrise and sunset, the fragile loveliness of a wisp of cloud fringed with silver, the wonder of day dawning and the delight of companionship—all these are His handiwork.

*God is with me.* Again and again I am stirred by some experience of tenderness, some simple act of gratuitous kindness moving from one man to another, some quiet deed of courage, wisdom or sacrifice or some striking movement of unstudied joy that bursts forth in the contagion of merry laughter. I know God is with me.

*God is with me.* Always there is the persistent need for some deep inner assurance, some whisper in my heart, some stirring of the spirit within me—that renews, re-creates and steadies. Then whatever betides of light or shadow, I can look out on life with quiet eyes.

God is with me.

## 25. Not Pity, but Compassion

God is at work enlarging the boundaries of my heart.
GOD is making room in my heart for compassion.

There is already a vast abundance of room for pity. It is often easy to be overcome with self-pity, that sticky substance that ruins everything it touches. My list of excuses is a long list and even as I say it, I know that under closest scrutiny they disappear, one by one. There is pity in me—pity for others. But there is something in it that cannot be trusted; it is mixed with pride, arrogance, cunning. I see this only when I expose myself to the eyes of God in the quiet time. It is now that I see what my pity really is and the sources from which it springs.

God is making room in my heart for compassion: the awareness that where my life begins is where your life begins; the awareness that the sensitiveness to your needs cannot be separated from the sensitiveness to my needs; the awareness that the joys of my heart are never mine alone—nor are my sorrows. I struggle against the work of God in my heart; I want to be let alone. I want my boundaries to remain fixed, that I may be at rest. But even now, as I turn to Him in the quietness, His work in me is ever the same.

God is at work enlarging the boundaries of my heart.

## 26. God is Present

*God is present with me this day.*

GOD is present with me in the midst of my anxieties. I affirm in my own heart and mind the reality of His presence. He makes immediately available to me the strength of His goodness, the reassurance of His wisdom and the heartiness of His courage. My anxieties are real; they are the result of a wide variety of experiences, some of which I understand, some of which I do not understand. One thing I know concerning my anxieties: they are real to me. Sometimes they seem more real than the presence of God. When this happens, they dominate my mood and possess my thoughts. The presence of God does not always deliver me from anxiety but it always delivers me from anxieties. Little by little, I am beginning to understand that deliverance from anxiety means fundamental growth in spiritual character and awareness. It becomes a quality of being, emerging from deep within, giving to all the dimensions of experience a vast immunity against being anxious. A ground of calm underlies experiences whatever may be the tempestuous character of events. This calm is the manifestation in life of the active, dynamic Presence of God.

*God is present with me this day.*

## 27. Myself, a High Priest of Truth

*I will make of my life a High Priest of Truth.*

I WILL make of my talents, whatever they are, a High Priest of Truth. This I do when I use them to enrich life, to render life more human, to make life more gracious and personal than it would be otherwise. I recognize that my talents may be special endowments or they may be the result of the advantageous path along which my life has come from the beginning.

I will make of my remembering a High Priest of Truth. I purpose in my heart that I shall not use my memory to store up those things which fester, poison and destroy my living, my life, or the living and the life of others. I shall make it my study to preserve my soul in balance and liberty. I will use my memory to store up the excellent things of my experience. In this way I shall lay up treasures in Heaven.

I will make of myself a High Priest of Truth. I will recognize the supremacy of the Ideal of Godlikeness to which more and more, by His help, I will give myself. Despite the number of times I fail, despite all the limitations and inadequacies which beset me, by God's strength I will make of myself a High Priest of Truth.

*I will make of my life a High Priest of Truth.*

## 28. Courage and Cowardice

THERE is ever a thin line which separates courage from cowardice. Sometimes the distinction between courage and cowardice is not easy to make. Here is a man who seems always to manifest bravery. Even before the issues are clearly defined, he takes his stand, lest he be regarded by himself or others as being a coward. Or, it may be that he moves into a situation with utter recklessness, unmindful of any clear estimate of what is involved, lest his deliberateness might be construed as a fearful hesitance. As a boy he was ever one to take a dare, because he did not want to seem "chicken." He is always first to sense a moment when an issue seems to be side-stepped and is ever eager to grasp the nettle while others wait for reinforcement. He enjoys the reputation of being forthright, direct and unafraid. This estimate of his fellows may be well deserved. But it may not be; for his seeming courage may be but his defense against a deep inner uncertainty and creeping fear. What he has not discovered is that of which true courage consists.

Courage is not a blustering manifestation of strength and power. Sometimes courage is only revealed in the midst of great weakness and greater fear. It is often the ultimate rallying of all the resources of personality to face a crucial and devastating demand. And this is not all. There is a quiet courage that comes from an inward spring of confidence in the meaning and significance of life. Such courage is an underground river, flowing far beneath the shifting events of one's experience, keeping alive a thousand little springs of action. It has neither trumpet to announce it nor crowds to applaud; it is best seen in the lives of men and women who do their work from day to day without hurry and without fever. It is the patient waiting of the humble man whose integrity keeps his spirit sweet and his heart strong. Wherever one encounters it, a lift is given to life and vast reassurance invades the being. To walk with such a person in the daily round is to keep company with angels, to have one's path illumined by the "Light that lighteth every man that cometh into the world."

## 29. Strength to be Free

"GIVE me the strength to be free." The thought of being free comes upon us sometimes with such power that under its impact we lose the meaning that the thought implies. Often, "being free" means to be where we are not at the moment, to be relieved of a particular set of chores or responsibilities that are bearing heavily upon minds, to be surrounded by a careless rapture with no reminders of costs of any kind, to be on the open road with nothing overhead but the blue sky and whole days in which to roam. For many, "being free" means movement, change, reordering.

To be free may not mean any of these things. It may not involve a single change in a single circumstance, or it may not extend beyond one's own gate, beyond the four walls in the midst of which all of one's working hours and endless nights

are spent. It may mean no surcease from the old familiar
routine and the perennial cares which have become one's persistent lot. Quite possibly, your days mean the deepening
of your rut, the increasing of your monotony and the enlarging of the areas of your dullness. All of this, and more, may
be true for you.

"Give me the strength to be free." Often, to be free means
the ability to deal with the realities of one's situation so as not
to be overcome by them. It is the manifestation of a quality of being and living that results not only from understanding of one's situation but also from wisdom in dealing
with it. It takes no strength to give up, to accept shackles
of circumstance so that they become shackles of soul, to shrug
the shoulders in bland acquiescence. This is easy. But do not
congratulate yourself that you have solved anything. In simple language, you have sold out, surrendered, given up. It
takes strength to affirm the high prerogative of your spirit.
And you will find that if you do, a host of invisible angels
will wing to your defense, and the glory of the living God
will envelop your surroundings because in you He has come
into His own.

## 30. The Embattled Spirit

O, THE agony of the embattled spirit in the anguished grapple
    with pride!
Pride of achievement, pride of bitterness—
Pride of the broken heart, pride of silent suffering

Pride of love and hatred
Pride of husband and wife
Pride of parent and child
Pride of class and race
Pride of nation and flag
Pride of righteousness and lust—

O, the agony of the embattled spirit in the anguished grapple
    with pride!
Teach us, our Father, the precious clue to honesty!
Grant that where we are, in what we do
Life need take no offense in us!
Search us, knead us, remove from us
The spots, the blemishes, even the shadows
That sent us forth in our own light
Shielded from Thy radiance and Thy fullness.


## 31. Let us Pray

SHE was an undergraduate chosen to take the prayer in the
Sunday service in the college chapel. With calmness and confidence she said quietly, "Let us pray." In a moment, all was
stillness—the very atmosphere of the chapel with its thirteen
hundred people became vibrant with a living Presence. It
moved over the congregation like a great noiseless wave. I
was no longer myself alone but I became one with a vast
company of worshipers in a timeless heartbeat before the
scrutiny of God. After the service, I asked her if she would

send me a copy of the prayer. To my great joy, she said, "Please take this. I would like you to have it." She handed me the following copy:

LET US PRAY

Our Father, Thou knowest our nature and readest our innermost thoughts, and nothing can be hidden from Thee; help us, then, to unburden ourselves of every disguise we wear before the world, and find strength in being what we are, Thy humble and grateful children. Enable us to put off sham and pretense. Be patient with any of us who still prefer vain shows and empty pride to the freedom and security of Thy Truth.

Enable us to carry out from this place peace and strength that here we gain. Because we have talked with Thee here, may we be able to work more patiently for Thy Kingdom, bringing light upon the problems that perplex the world, dispelling the night of doubt and fear with Thy sheltering love.                    Amen.

In pencil she had written:

*Be sure to pray!*

## 32. The Patience of Unanswered Prayer

"TEACH me the patience of unanswered prayer" is a line of the familiar hymn. It opens up before the mind the wide intensity of unfulfilled hopes, broken dreams and anguished denials. Who is there that has not carried at a central place in his concerns the persistent hunger, sometimes dull and quiet, sometimes feverish and angry, for something that has not come to pass. The hunger moves in the background of all the days like the rumble of distant thunder or the far-off roar of the sea. Sometimes it is so close that all of life seems summarized in its urgency and its denial, the denial of life itself.

The general overtones of anguish created by the unfulfilled need often send the soul searching for some clue, some key to unlock the door of the treasure house. All sorts of things are tried. Often there is the searching of one's own way of life to see if in the intricacies of the personal behavior pattern may not stand revealed the reason for the unmet need. Often there is the subtle intimation of some weakness in the character that takes no overt form but turns up as limitations in understanding or blind spots in perception. Often there is the sure knowledge that one has been hurt, crippled by the actions of others and no care was excrcised in the healing process, with the result that growth was out of line and twisted. But despite all of the meaning of all of the possible clues, the persistent hunger works away deep within. It remains unfulfilled and unmet.

Slowly it may dawn upon the spirit that there is a special ministry of unfulfillment. It may be that the persistent hunger is an Angel of Light, carrying out a particular assignment in life. With the coming of this possibility into consideration, slowly, tensions are relaxed and the center of emphasis is shifted from the hunger itself to what it has meant to deal with it through all the years. Slowly at first, the words are shaped and the pattern of them shows itself. At last, a man may say, "I know now that there is present in my life a quality that is only mine because the hunger is mine. Thus, at last, I come to the door and seek entrance where is gathered the great community. I know the password: 'Teach me the patience of unanswered prayer.'"

# II

## *The Binding Ties*

There is a curious logic in human experience that finally permits no man to escape the good and the bad. Often the event in which the individual is involved seems to carry with it an order which is independent of merit or demerit. This indeterminateness seems to suggest that in all living there is an element which may be regarded as *random* in the sense that it is outside of an orderly pattern of reaping and sowing. To be alive is to be involved in events, some of which take their rise uniquely in the individual's experience and some of which flow into the life, apparently without rhyme or reason. To accept all experience as raw material out of which the human spirit distills meanings and values is a part of the meaning of maturity.

## 1. Life Seems Unaware

ONCE again the smell of death rides on the winds
  And fear lurks within the shadows of the mind.
One by one the moments tick away.
  Days and nights are interludes
Between despairing hope and groping faith.
  Of this bleak desolation, Life seems unaware:
Seeds still die and live again in answer to their kind;
  Fledgling birds awake to life from prison house of shell;
Flowers bloom and blossoms fall as harbingers of fruit to
      come;
  The newborn child comes even on the wings of death;
The thoughts of men are blanketed by dreams
  Of tranquil days and peaceful years,
When love unfettered will keep the heart and mind
  In ways of life that crown our days with light.


## 2. Struggle Is an Aspect of Life

AGAIN and again we seek to escape from the struggle of life. It is perfectly normal to long for, yea, even to seek some quiet retreat from the struggle in which we engage constantly. One need hardly be ashamed of such feelings and desires. Sometimes the struggle has to do with the matter of earning a living, of keeping alive with some measure of dignity and decency. Often it has to do with a total series of relationships, personal or impersonal. Or again, it may have to do with the fight for life against the ravages of some insidious disease. In its most dramatic form it may have to do with some inner temptation, some profound battle or the will to do with one's own spirit that which seems to be the right, when some easier way looms large on the horizon. The interesting thing to remember is, one's own struggle is individual but it is not unique. All of life is involved—in fact, struggle is an inescapable aspect of life itself. A friend described the emergence of a sea gull from its egg. The process took many hours. There was the incessant pecking away at the shell from the inside. The rhythm of the sound was interrupted by occasional noises of apparent distress and anguish. But always the pecking—hour after hour—until at last the shell cracked from the inside. Then the bird emerged, wet, bedraggled— it did not get dry for many additional hours. One has seen a butterfly emerge from its fibrous prison house. What struggle, what tempestuous effort! The struggle of man seems to be more marked because man knows that he is struggling, which means that he must struggle even as he abides the thought of a struggle—a double portion. This double struggle is underscored by the difference between the private ends of the individual and the impersonal purposes and forces that surround him. But there is always strength for struggle. The sure knowledge of the fact gives wings to the spirit even when the struggle is deepest. It is the insistence of religion that the God of life and the God of religion are one and the same. Implicit in the struggle which is a part of life is the vitality that life itself supplies. To affirm this with all of one's passionate endeavor is to draw deeply upon the resource available to anyone who dares to draw upon it. The aliveness of life and the power of God move through the same channel at the point of greatest need and awareness. What precious ingredients!

## 3. At My Center I Find Peace

How to get beyond one's anxiety and trouble to the center of one's own spirit is one of the most formidable hurdles to serenity and inner peace. To say that it is perfectly human or natural is not to get relief from the turmoil. Again and again, a man tries to pray, tries to penetrate the mist, only to find that he loses his way and lands back in the arms of his anxiety. At the moment, it is impossible to get through; he cannot even keep his mind in focus long enough to center it upon God. Always alternatives, solutions to his troubles, appear and reappear, the same ones, in an endless series which he has already examined a thousand times. The experience is like a cracked record, the needle stays put and round and round the record goes, repeating the same phrase. In despair he is tempted to give up seeking, to yield at last to the overwhelming power of his deep anxiety. He may say to himself, "I am not going to think about it any more. By sheer act of will, I shall dismiss the whole thing from my mind." But even as he says this, he knows that it is not so easy or so simple as that. It may be that a man can fill his mind with

positive thoughts about his distress. When he does this, he
realizes that, repeatedly, his thoughts seem to bounce off
the top of his anxiety, unable to penetrate and resolve it.
Some way must be found by which his distress can be
destroyed, washed away or uprooted. It is obvious that it has
a source, a cause or a root. It did not just happen! Too, the
cause may have long since disappeared, only the effect remains, which in turn becomes a fresh cause, keeping alive the
mainsprings of distress. One possible cure is to get to the root
of it and dig it out. Rich indeed is the testimony of the
efficacy of that kind of treatment.

If such be my experience, then I can get to my center. I can
find peace or, better still, peace finds me and I give myself
to it with deep joy and tranquillity.

There is still another way by which the masses of humanity
through all the ages have taken the hurdles of their distresses.
Sometimes with magic, sometimes by way of the grossest
kind of superstitions, they find a means by which to turn
themselves *and* their distress over to a power conceived to be
greater than themselves. When this has been accomplished,
there is relief and peace. What the folk spirit has discerned
through ages of living and struggling becomes the core of
the self-conscious procedure of the deeply religious man or
woman. For such, this is not a single act but a thing that may
be done over and over until, at last, peace has come. Therefore, if a man cannot give his anxiety to God that he may at
last get to his own center which is his tryst with Him, he may
be able to give to God the *total* operation including himself.
This is the testimony of many. Is it yours?

## 4. Pain Has a Ministry

MANY years ago life was characterized by a great poet as a vale of soulmaking; the basic notion being that all of the experiences of living have as a single purpose the growth (perhaps the creation) and the development of the soul of man. That is, the development of a quality in human life that would give to all the rest of living a sensitiveness, a depth of being, which would put man in the fullest possession of all his powers; in other words, make man whole. There is a quiet strength in such a picture because it takes the dread out of the painful and the tragic aspects of living. It is not unreasonable to assume that men are enriched and joyed by the good and the beautiful and the satisfying. Men can accustom themselves to such things as their due or as a part of the gifts of life to the children of men. But what about pain, what about the hardships, the things that make for misery? It is perhaps a daring notion to say that pain has a ministry which adds to the sum total of life's meaning and, more importantly, to its fulfillment. And yet, through all the ages of the life of man, this idea has kept pace with the growth of mind. There is a ministry of pain and the poet suggests indirectly that its ministry is the making of the souls of men. But in this idea lies a very certain danger: namely, that specific pain is sent into the life to perform a ministry in the life of the individual. This idea is current among those who say in the presence of tragedy, "We bow humbly before the will of God." But this idea is deadly because it yields the mind to a kind of fatalism of despair and futility which stunts the spirit and destroys the basic faith in the goodness and the wisdom of God. It is necessary, therefore, to distinguish between the ministry of pain in general and that of a particular circumstance. Concerning the ministry of pain, it can be said that any tragedy has inherent in it positive good. One is not under any necessity to discover this fact but one may. And this is important to remember: given the fact of pain as a normal part of the experience of life, one may make the pain contribute to the soul, to the life meaning. One may be embittered, ground down by it, but one need not be. The pain of life may teach us to understand life and, in our understanding of life, to love life. To love life truly is to be whole in all one's parts; and to be whole in all one's parts is to be free and unafraid.

## 5. All Men Live the Eternal

EVERY person must of necessity deal with the fact of death. There is no escape. There are three basic attitudes which men take toward this aspect of universal experience. One attitude is to dread it; another is to ignore it; and still another is to accept it. Perhaps dread is the most prevailing attitude. The reasons for this are not far to seek. In some important ways, death means the end of many things. The whole range of activities and functions that have characterized what is generally meant by life are stopped, cut off, finished. One by one, the duties end; one by one, the lights go out. The delicate network of relations by which an individual defines the meaning and significance of his own person is ruptured. All this is contemplated with a kind of uneasiness of spirit which underscores the essential solitariness of all living. It is for this reason that death is often characterized as the long march, the silent journey, the last lonely mile. The essential solitariness of life for the individual gives an important clue to the searching answer to the dread of death. This privacy remains untouched because it is outside of, and not involved in, any event. It would seem that both life and death take place outside the central core of the spirit of the individual. This means that life, measured in terms of events, of happenings, of shifts and changes, affects only the superficial or surface part of the individual's living. But life in another sense goes on simultaneously and is unaffected by all the happenings, whatever may be their character. In this sense, death is something that comes *in* life but not something that comes *to* life. This is the meaning of the eternal in time. All men live the eternal in time. But not all men are aware of this aspect of their lives. One of the great insights of religion is that men who live at this deeper level know eternal life, in time. Here is one of the central insistences of Jesus, that death is powerless over the life of a man who lives the eternal in time. The true meaning is not that man does not die as the grass dies. When he realizes that at his very core he is a part of life in a private, personal, intimate sense and that that privacy is never invaded, then he contemplates all change, however seemingly fundamental, as truly external to him. In such contemplation, birth and death, with all the vicissitudes in between, are but episodes in a wide range of possibilities. From such a point of view, one may look forward to death not with dread but with the kind of anticipation which any new experience arouses in the mind of the adventurous spirit.

## 6. Who, or What, is to Blame?

THE desire to be one's true self is ever persistent. Equally persistent is the tendency to locate the responsibility for failure to be one's true self in events, persons and conditions—all of which are outside and beyond one's self. Often a person says, "I would be the kind of person I desire to be," or "I would do the thing that I have always wanted to do *if*—." The list is endless: if I had been born a boy rather than a girl; if I had been tall and strong rather than short and weak; if I had been given the diet proper for a growing child; if my parents had been understanding and sympathetic rather than cold and impersonal, thereby giving to me the feeling of being rejected; if I had lived in a different kind of community, or had grown up on the right side of the tracks; if my parents had not separated when I was but a child and made me the victim of a broken home; if I had not been taught the wrong things about sex, about religion, about myself; if I had been of a different racial or national origin—and on and on. The interesting fact is, that in each "if" there is apt to be, for the person who uses it, a significant element of truth. This element of truth is seized upon as the complete answer to the personal problem, as the single source of all the individual's maladjustments.

There is more to the story than is indicated. Often, not always, the person who feels most completely defeated in fulfillment is the one who has been unable or unwilling to exploit resources that were close at hand. There is a curious inability to take personal responsibility for what one does or fails to do, without a sense of martyrdom or heroics. Religion is most helpful in developing in the individual a sense of personal responsibility for one's action and thus aiding the process of self-fulfillment. It is helpful in two ways primarily: There is the insistence upon the individual's responsibility to God for his own life. This means that he cannot escape the scrutiny of God. If he is responsible to God, the basis of that responsibility has to be in himself. If it is there, then the area of alibis is definitely circumscribed. The assumption is that the individual is ever in immediate candidacy to get an "assist" from God—that he is not alone in his quest. Through prayer, meditation and singleness of mind, the individual's life may be invaded by strength, insight and courage sufficient for his needs. Thus he need not seek refuge in excuses but can live his life with ever-increasing vigor and experience . . . an ever-deepening sense of fulfillment.

## 7. Our Children are not *Things*

IT IS in order to think about children and our relationship to them. Often we underestimate both our influence and our responsibility with reference to children because they do not seem to be mindful of our presence except in terms of something to resist. The world of the adult is in some ways a different world from that of the child. We bring to bear upon life the cumulative judgment garnered from our years of living, of trial and error, of many, many discoveries along the way. It is from that kind of context that we judge the behavior of children. But they have not lived and there is much that can be known and understood only from the harvest of the years. This fact should not blind us to the profound way in which we determine even in detail the attitudes and the very structure of the child's thought. If we are good to the child and to other people, he will get from us directly a conception of goodness more profound and significant than all the words we may use about goodness as an ideal. If we lose our temper and give way to hard, brittle words which we fling around and about, the child learns more profoundly and significantly than all the formal teaching about self-control which may be offered him. If we love a child, and the child senses from our relationship with others that we love them, he will get a concept of love that all the subsequent hatred in the world will never be quite able to destroy. It is idle to teach the child formally about respect for other people or other groups if in little ways we demonstrate that we have no authentic respect for other people and other groups. The feeling tone and insight of the child are apt to be unerring. It is not important whether the child is able to comprehend the words we use or understand the ideas that we make articulate. The child draws his *meaning* from the meaning which we put into things that we do and say. Let us not be deceived. We may incorporate in our formal planning all kinds of ideas for the benefit of the children. We may provide them with tools of various kinds. But if there is not genuineness in our climate, if in little ways we regard them as nuisances, as irritations, as *things* in the way of our pursuits, they will know that we do not love them and that our religion has no contagion for them. Let us gather around our children and give to them the security that can come only from associating with adults who mean what they say and who share in deeds which are broadcast in words.

## 8. Let Your Words be Yea and Nay

ONE of the most incisive stories told by Jesus concerned a man who had two sons. To the first he said, "Son, go work today in the vineyard." Very quickly, the son responded by saying that he would not do it. Then Jesus adds, "but afterward he repented and went." To the other son he made the same request. Immediately he responded by saying that he would oblige his father, but did not do so. The point of the story expressed in the gospel is, that the son who said "No" but changed his mind, did the will of his father. It is a very interesting picture presented here concerning one whose immediate reaction to any request is negative. It does not matter how simple the request is or how complicated, the spontaneous reply is in the negative. A very commonplace adage, descriptive of such a personality is: His bark is worse than his bite. Such persons are never so negative as their words would indicate. This may be a matter of temperament. Once this particular characteristic is understood, it is easy to depend upon their carrying through in positive terms the things to which they had reacted negatively. Sometimes such persons start a trend in the wrong direction when their first words influence others who will abide by the negative judgment. The function of such an attitude may be to screen all proposals first by challenging their validity and their claims, and denial may quickly lay bare the integrity of the proposal. Such may be a timesaver in the end. I wonder. The other boy may be characterized as "Mr. Facing-both-ways"—one of the figures in *Pilgrim's Progress*. His attitude seems to be to give no offense—to agree but to reverse for oneself the true intent. For some such persons, it is an inability to say "No." The result is that such a boy may be pushed by anything, anytime, anywhere, with no moral integrity to bottom the argument. Here is a character weakness, because it places at a discount the value of the word. The word is the symbol, the communication symbol of meaning, of intent, of purpose. If the symbol is fundamentally unreliable, then the basis of relations becomes at once chaotic and often immoral. At another place in the gospels the words of Jesus are of a different sort—"Let your words be yea, yea, and nay, nay." Simple but terribly difficult—quite possible but searching.

## 9. Thank God for Humor!

THERE is always in every human relationship and in every private life some place for humor, for the sparkle in the water of life. It is easy to understand the reason for much of the tension that engulfs us. Sometimes we take our own lives so seriously that there is scarcely room on the planet for any other life. There is a sense in which our own problems loom so large that they dominate our entire horizon, and all there is for us to think and feel is that which is central to our particular burdens. We may, all of us, have our moments when it seems that life is taking out all of its grievances upon us, that others around us are permitted to make their purchases at life's bargain counters while we are forced to pay and pay and pay all that the traffic can bear, and more. If this be our mood then there is no antidote quite like a central chuckle of the spirit. Humor may not be laughter, it may not even be a smile; it is primarily a point of view, an attitude toward experience—a tangent. It requires a certain quality of objectivity—the inspired ability to step aside and see one's self go by. To take in the total view is to establish perspective, and many things fall into place. What is extra, what does not belong, becomes the source of the overtone, the chuckle that restores the balance. There is nothing superficial here; there is no cruelty, as is indicated when humor becomes a weapon to embarrass and attack persons. True humor is a weapon, but it is used creatively when it is held firmly in the hands of a man who uses it against himself and his own antics. All the gods of depression, gloom and melancholy must shriek with alarm when there rings down the corridor the merry music of the humorous spirit. It means that fear is in rout, that there is deep understanding of the process of life and an expansive faith which advises the spirit that, because life is its own restraint, life can be trusted. What a deadly religion if it has no humor—what a dreary life where that precious venture has not emerged. Thank God for humor!

## 10. To What Loyalty are You True?

It is never quite possible to resolve in a manner that is completely satisfying the conflict between loyalties. There is the conflict between loyalty to the ideal of mercy on the one hand and loyalty to the ideal of literal truthtelling on the other. In Henry van Dyke's story, *The Other Wise Man,* there is an account of one experience which the Other Wise Man had with Herod's soldiers. He came to a court within which was a cottage. When he entered the cottage he found a young woman and her male child hiding in a corner. Herod had dispatched his soldiers to kill all male children under a certain age. When the leader of a small group of soldiers appeared at the door of the cottage, he asked the Other Wise Man, "Is there a male child in this house?" Whereupon the reply came back directly: "No." And the child's life was spared. If you had been at the door, to which loyalty would you have been true? Perhaps, if it were your own child there would be no question. I wonder. Or consider the conflict between loyalty to an ultimate goal and loyalty to an immediate goal, both of which are good but one seems to be better than the other, though more remote. The platitude, A bird in the hand is worth two in the bush, is one answer. How often do we seize upon the immediate good because it is within reach and thereby sacrifice the better thing because the time interval is so great that we fear we shall die before we realize it! To escape the risk of losing all, we accept what is available. The issue becomes clearer when we apply it to a concrete situation. A man runs for a political office. Standing outside of the responsibility of the office, it is clear to him what is the right, the ideal thing to do. When he is elected, he becomes a man with the responsibility of office and, all his days, he wrestles with the loyalty to his ideals and loyalty to the responsibilities of office. Power always involves a man in a network of compromises. This is true because a man has to be selfless in relation to his ideals or be destroyed by them. Power always includes more than the private relation between a man and his personal ideals. To give up the struggle is to lose one's soul. And what would a man give in exchange for his soul? Fame? Prestige? Glory? Power?

## 11. Relations to Others Must Be Dynamic

WE LIVE under the constant pressure of the demands and expectations of other people. There is scarcely any person who escapes the feeling that someone or some group or some event is breathing down his neck. This feeling of pressure begins early in life, usually when we are very, very young. The most natural thing in the world is, that we should want to please and to be pleasing. It is a part of the process by which we become human beings. It is a part of the effort, the creative effort, of relating ourselves meaningfully to those

of our immediate family or group. In this experiencing of
related and being related, we are apt to focus our efforts on
a single person, usually a particular parent. There may be
many reasons for this situation. When such is our experience,
we become primarily or secondarily dominated by the necessity to please, and be pleasing to, the parent or the substitute:
a friend, a wife, a husband, a job, a child, a profession—
there are all kinds of substitutes. Our scale of values and
our sense of morality are apt to be measured in such terms.
Right or wrong, praise or blame, success or failure—all are
determined in part by the things that thicken or rupture the
line of our relatedness to our object.

There is nothing out of line about the experience we have
been describing so long as it remains fluid and chronolog-
ically contemporary. The danger is in the fact that, while in
various ways we continue growing and developing and experiencing, the point of our most fundamental sense of
relatedness may be fixed. We try to overcome this by the
ruse of substitutes, but the character of the relatedness remains the same. It would seem that, in order for growth to
be continuous and healthy rather than continuous and malig-
nant, it is important that the character of our relatedness be
and remain dynamic. It must grow and grow, to the end that
it will be a true expression of our living experience at the
time. What will be demanded of us under such circumstances
will be one with what we truly demand of ourselves. Ultimately, the meaning of religious experience in the life of
the person is, that all of the points at which he is related are

God-substitutes. God has made us for Himself, is the way this is phrased in the language of religion.

## 12. The World is too Much With Us

THE problem of the religious man's attitude toward the world is persistent and perennial. One reaches a conclusion about it only to discover that it becomes unresolved again. Perhaps the most direct attempt toward a solution is to seek withdrawal from the world. "The world is too much with us"—is a common feeling. When one seeks withdrawal from the world, it is admission that the world is fundamentally and completely "other than" that which is congenial to the things of the spirit; or the individual who seeks withdrawal is convinced that, for his highest spiritual growth, he must not be involved in the entanglements which are the common lot. If it is the former, the inescapable conclusion is that the contradictions of experience are in themselves final and binding. There is ever a recognition of the necessity of temporary withdrawal from the world and its insistences. This is a part of the very rhythm of life. We live by alternations. The religious man is no exception. He withdraws from the world, and then he attacks the world; he retreats and he advances.

Or the religious man may summarize all that the world means in terms of negations into one single manifestation. He may decide that all evil, for instance, is reduced to a single entity. It may be alcohol, or tobacco, or war, or greed. If such is his conclusion, then it follows that all energies must be bent toward a single end. Such a solution to the problems of the world is, perhaps, a radical oversimplification. It says that, from within the confines of a particular manifestation of the world, the total solution to the problem of life must be sought and may be found. Obviously, such a solution is inadequate. Both religion and life are too complex—and personality indeed.

Or the religious man may recognize that all the world is made up of raw materials which stand in immediate candidacy for the realization of the kingdom, the rule of God. This is a very far-reaching insight with profound radical implications. The idea is inherent in the suggestion to Peter in *The Acts of the Apostles* that nothing that God made should be regarded as unclean. If God is the Creator of life in its totality, then all things are in candidacy for the achievement of the high and holy end. This is not to say that evil has no meaning, but it is to say that, once the evilness of evil is removed, resolved, uprooted, then the total character is thoroughly altered. The religious man who takes this position is never afraid of life, nor does he shrink from vicissitudes. He seeks at every point the emergence of the will and the mind of God from within himself and within the stuff of life itself. What is revealed in life is one with that which transcends life.

## 13. Every Man Must Decide

THE ability to know what is the right thing to do in a given circumstance is a sheer gift of God. The element of gift is inherent in the process of decision. Perhaps gift is the wrong word; it is a quality of genius or immediate inspiration. The process is very simple and perhaps elemental. First, we weigh all the possible alternatives. We examine them carefully, weighing this and weighing that. There is always an abundance of advice available—some of it technical, some of it out of the full-orbed generosity of those who love us and wish us well. Each bit of it has to be weighed and measured in the light of the end sought. This means that the crucial consideration is to know what is the desirable end. What is it that I most want to see happen if the conditions were ideal or if my desire were completely fulfilled? Once this end is clearly visualized, then it is possible to have a sense of direction with reference to the decision that must be made. If it becomes clear that the ideal end cannot be realized, it follows that such a pursuit has to be relinquished. This relinquishment is always difficult because the mind, the spirit, the body desires are all focused upon the ideal end. Every person thinks that it is his peculiar destiny to have the ideal come true for him. The result is that, with one's mind, the ideal possibility is abandoned but emotionally it is difficult to give it up. Thus the conflict. The resources of one's personality cannot be marshaled. A man finds that he cannot work wholeheartedly for the achievable or possible end because he cannot give up the inner demand for the ideal end. Oftentimes precious months or years pass with no solution in evidence because there is ever the hope that the ideal end may, in some miraculous manner, come to pass. Then the time for action does come at last. There comes a moment when something has to be done; one can no longer postpone the decision—the definite act resolves an otherwise intolerable situation. Once the decision is made, the die is cast. Is my decision right or wrong, wise or foolish? At the moment, I may be unable to answer the question. For what is right in the light of the present set of facts may not be able to stand up under the scrutiny of unfolding days. I may not have appraised the facts properly. My decision may have been largely influenced by my desires which were at work at the very center of my conscious processes. In the face of all the uncertainties that surround any decision, the wise man acts in the light of his best judgment illumined by the integrity of his profoundest spiritual insights. Then the rest is in the hands of the future and in the mind of God. The possibility of error, of profound and terrible error, is at once the height and the depth of man's freedom. For this, God be praised!

## 14. Enthusiasm and Self-sacrifice

IN THE preface to the first English edition of *The Philosophy of Civilization*, Albert Schweitzer says that nothing of real value in the world is ever accomplished without enthusiasm and self-sacrifice. Literally, the word "enthusiasm" means "God-possessed." Under certain circumstances, a man is moved to action and to feelings that are more than his customary actions and feelings. Something happens to him, there is a plus to his normal energy and powers. The relationship is intimate between enthusiasm and morale. Morale is belief in one's cause, one's purpose, one's self. Out of the surplus generated by enthusiasm, morale is fashioned.

The other term to be examined is "self-sacrifice." It is the judgment upon an act that is past, a deed that is done. It is a reflection upon a meaning that was not evident in the act itself. I realize that what I have done has involved me in choices that would not have been necessary were it not for the commitment which sent me forth. Of course, there are times when a man decides deliberately to yield something that is of intense personal meaning to himself in order that he may be free of it and thereby able to do something else more effectively. In any such decision, that which has been given up has been sacrificed. There are times when a man gives up his rest, his peace of mind, his health, his personal ambition, his security and even his very life, because of his enthusiasm for something else which he holds more significant than whether he lives or dies. Whenever we are in the presence of such nobility, such grandeur of spirit, we are caught up in the magic of its power. It is literally true, as Schweitzer suggests, that nothing of real value in the world is ever accomplished without enthusiasm and self-sacrifice.

## 15. The Seed of the Jack Pine

IN RESPONSE to a letter of inquiry addressed to a Canadian forester concerning the jack pine which abounds in British Columbia, the following statement was received: "Essentially, you are correct when you say that jack pine cones require artificial heat to release the seed from the cone. The cones often remain closed for years, the seeds retaining their viability. In the interior of the province, the cones which have dropped to the ground will open at least partly with the help of the sun's reflected heat. However, the establishment of the majority of our jack pine stands has undoubtedly been established following forest fires. Seldom do the cones release their seed while on the tree."

The seed of the jack pine will not be given up by the cone unless the cone itself is subjected to sustained and concentrated heat. The forest fire sweeps all before it and there remain but the charred reminders of a former growth and a former beauty. It is then in the midst of the ashes that the secret of the cone is exposed. The tender seed finds the stirring of life deep within itself—and what is deepest in the seed reaches out to what is deepest in life—the result? A tender shoot, gentle roots, until, at last, there stands straight against the sky the majestic glory of the jack pine.

It is not too far afield to suggest that there are things deep within the human spirit that are firmly imbedded, dormant, latent and inactive. These things are always positive, even though they may be destructive rather than creative. But there they remain until our lives are swept by the forest fire: It may be some mindless tragedy, some violent disclosure of human depravity or some moment of agony in which the whole country or nation may be involved. The experience releases something that has been locked up within all through the years. If it be something that calls to the deepest things in life, we may, like the jack pine, grow tall and straight against the sky!

## 16. Our Little Lives

OUR little lives, our big problems—these we place upon Thy altar!

The quietness in Thy Temple of Silence again and again rebuffs us:

For some there is no discipline to hold them steady in the waiting

And the minds reject the noiseless invasion of Thy Spirit.

For some there is no will to offer what is central in the thoughts—

The confusion is so manifest, there is no starting place to take hold.

For some the evils of the world tear down all concentrations

And scatter the focus of the high resolves.

> War and the threat of war has covered us with heavy shadows,
> Making the days big with forebodings—

The nights crowded with frenzied dreams and
   restless churnings.
We do not know how to do what we know to do.
We do not know how to be what we know to be.

Our little lives, our big problems—these we place upon Thy
   altar!
Brood over our spirits, Our Father,
Blow upon whatever dream Thou hast for us
That there may glow once again upon our hearths
The light from Thy altar.
Pour out upon us whatever our spirits need of shock, of lift,
   of release
That we may find strength for these days—
Courage and hope for tomorrow.
In confidence we rest in Thy sustaining grace
Which makes possible triumph in defeat, gain in loss, and
   love in hate.
We rejoice this day to say:
Our little lives, our big problems—these we place upon Thy
   altar!


## 17. When the Strain is Heaviest

AT TIMES when the strain is heaviest upon us,
And our tired nerves cry out in many-tongued pain
Because the flow of love is choked far below the deep recesses
   of the heart,

We seek with cravings firm and hard
The strength to break the dam
That we may live again in love's warm stream.
We want more love; and more and more
Until, at last, we are restored and made anew!
Or, so it seems.

When we are closer drawn to God's great Light
And in its radiance stand revealed,
The meaning of our need informs our minds.
"More love," we cried; as if love could be weighed, meas-
    ured, bundled, tied.
As if with perfect wisdom we could say—to one, a little love;
    to another, an added portion;
And on and on until all debts were paid
With no one left behind.

But now we see the tragic blunder of our cry.
Not for more love our hungry cravings seek!
But more power to love.
To put behind the tender feeling, the understanding heart,
The boundless reaches of the Father's Care
Makes love eternal, always kindled, always new.
This becomes the eager meaning of the aching heart
The bitter cry—the anguish call!

## 18. Reservoir or Canal

ARE you a reservoir or are you a canal or a swamp? The distinction is literal. The function of a canal is to channel water; it is a device by which water may move from one place to another in an orderly and direct manner. It holds water in a temporary sense only; it holds it in transit from one point to another. The function of the reservoir is to contain, to hold water. It is a large receptacle designed for the purpose, whether it is merely an excavation in the earth or some vessel especially designed. It is a place in which water is stored in order that it may be available when needed. In it provisions are made for outflow and inflow.

A swamp differs from either. A swamp has an inlet but no outlet. Water flows into it but there is no provision made for water to flow out. The result? The water rots and many living things die. Often there is a strange and deathlike odor that pervades the atmosphere. The water is alive but apt to be rotten. There is life in a swamp but it is stale.

The dominant trend of a man's life may take on the characteristics of a canal, reservoir or swamp. The important accent is on the dominant trend. There are some lives that seem ever to be channels, canals through which things flow. They are connecting links between other people, movements, purposes. They make the network by which all kinds of communications are possible. They seem to be adept at relating needs to sources of help, friendlessness to friendliness.

Of course, the peddler of gossip is also a canal. If you are a canal, what kind of things do you connect?

Or are you a reservoir? Are you a resource which may be drawn upon in times of others' needs and your own as well? Have you developed a method for keeping your inlet and your outlet in good working order so that the cup which you give is never empty? As a reservoir, you are a trustee of all the gifts God has shared with you. You know they are not your own.

Are you a swamp? Are you always reaching for more and more, hoarding whatever comes your way as your special belongings? If so, do you wonder why you are friendless, why the things you touch seem ever to decay? A swamp is a place where living things often sicken and die. The water in a swamp has no outlet. Canal, reservoir or swamp—WHICH?

## 19. Concerning the Yucca

A VERY kind friend sent me a letter a few days ago from which I quote the following: "I learned a truth about the Yucca . . . that its huge seed-pod cluster must never be disturbed until the pods are empty of seed . . . otherwise the seeds will be spilled on the rock and hard soil and be eaten by birds or mice. Only the terrific lashing and tearing of winter storms can rightly thrash out these seeds and smash them or their pods down among the rocks and thus blow or wash the seeds into crevices—where they can safely ger-

minate, root and find sufficient water and depth in their short
growing season before the summer drought sets in, thus to
carry over the young plant."

It is ever a dangerous thing to draw analogies. Nevertheless, the fact is inescapable that there are qualities that seem
to be hidden deep within the very texture of the human
spirit that can only be laid bare, that they may grow and be
fruitful, by the most terrific flailings of a desperate adversity.
There are not only such qualities as endurance but also such
qualities as tenderness, gentleness and boundless affection.
It seems that these qualities emerge in their fullest glory only
when there is nothing more that adversity can do. There is a
strange halo surrounding great tribulation which shines in
a transcendent glory. This radiance is the basis of the moral
appeal always inherent in profound suffering. In addition,
there is a starkness which suggests that an ultimate something has been reached which is eternal. The prophet on the
Isle of Patmos, in his vision, speaks of those who have gone
through great tribulation and that God shall wipe away every
tear from their eyes. It is the revelation of a dimension of the
human spirit that only becomes available when everything
else has been torn away. It is true that in the process everything may be swept away, but the testimony of countless
persons in all ages is that it is possible for a man to stand
anything that life can do to him. In those to whom such a
disclosure is made, the light of the eternal burns steadily and
undimmed. They have won the right; and theirs is the glory!

## 20. The Temptation to Oversimplify

THERE is ever present the temptation to reduce all problems to a single problem; to seize upon a single explanation for all the ills of life. In *Moby Dick*, Ahab reduces all evil to a single evil, the white whale. The white whale became to him the symbol of everything that was wrong in his experience, everything that was negative. If he could destroy the whale, then all evil would be destroyed. This is a common malady. As we contemplate our own lot, we can very easily single out a single circumstance which becomes for us the key to all our difficulties. We say, if I could get a job that I like, if I could live in another kind of place, if I had more money, if I could get rid of the pain in my back—if—if—if—then all my problems would be solved. Or again, we may think of all our experiences in terms that single out a particular virtue which becomes for us the ONE virtue in all of life. The ridiculous expression of this idea was voiced once by a man who said the resolution to all the problems of our age is a good five-cent cigar. If we could just get a good five-cent cigar, this would be a good world.

It is a common remark now that what we need is integration. Our generation is made up of neurotics because we are not integrated. Such a point of view regards integration as one single but total experience of personality. We forget that when we seek integration it is always with reference to some aspect of our lives. A man is never integrated. But rather, he is integrated as to some particular aspect of his life experience.

Life is simple but always complex. Human life is simple but ever complex. There cannot be single solutions that are in themselves total, because not only are we living organisms embodying varied stages of growth, development and experience at any particular moment, but life is also alive, complex and dynamic. There is no single evil but there are *evils*. It is hard to escape the necessity for singling out a particular thing and making it the symbol of all frustrations or all resolutions. When a man addressed Jesus, "Good Master, what shall I do?" Jesus replied, "Why callest thou me good? There is none good but God."

## 21. The Desert Dweller

HE HAS lived in the desert so long that all of its moods have long since become a part of the daily rhythm of his life. But it is not that fact that is of crucial importance. For many years, it has been his custom to leave a lighted lantern by the roadside at night to cheer the weary traveler. Beside the lantern, there is a note which gives detailed directions as to where his cottage may be found so that if there is distress or need, the stranger may find help. It is a very simple gesture full of beauty and wholeness. To him, it is not important who the stranger may be, it is not important how many people pass in the night and go on their way. The important thing is that the lantern burns every night and every night the note is there, "just in case."

Years ago, walking along a road outside Rangoon, I noted

at intervals along the way a roadside stone with a crock of water and, occasionally, some fruit. Water and fruit were put there by Buddhist priests to comfort and bless any passerby—one's spiritual salutation to another. The fact that I was a traveler from another part of the world, speaking a strange language and practicing a different faith, made no difference. What mattered was the fact that I was walking along the road—what my mission was, who I was—all irrelevant.

In your own way, do you keep a lantern burning by the roadside with a note saying where you may be found, "just in case?" Do you place a jar of cool water and a bit of fruit under a tree at the road's turning, to help the needy traveler? God knows the answer and so do you!


## 22. The Iron Lung

IT WAS my first contact with an iron lung. I had never been close to one before. What a stirring experience to stand before this miracle of human engineering and to become, in some measure, aware of the tremendous boon which it is to man. But the most moving aspect of my experience was the encounter with the young woman whose life had been saved by the steady ebb and flow of air as the sturdy bellows swished its sustaining currents to the paralyzed lungs. For more than a year the iron case had been bed and chair. All the days, moment by moment, were held together by the vital power of a single electric current. But in her face there was no trace of awareness of the tiny margin by which her life was spared. I sat in a chair facing the mirror into which she looked to see my face. When introductions were made, there was a long and searching look—eye met eye and held—then a quiet smile spread over her face. Suddenly and indescribably I felt like a child—as if all my days had been lived in shallow waters and that the profound meaning and the mystery of life had passed me by. I did not want to talk because here was the time to listen, to learn, to drink deep from the underground river that feeds and sustains not merely the life of man but life itself. It is curious how one's cup may be filled by another and no words are passed to indicate the process that is taking place. At last, the time came for me to leave. I said, "If I am in your city again, I hope I shall be privileged to visit you." Her reply, "You had better not make it too long or else you will not find me here. It will not be much longer now and I shall shed this and be well again." And why not? Her clinical picture indicated that she should have died months ago. As I went down the elevator, there was a new song in my heart and so great a sense of thanksgiving to God that I did not even try to keep back the tears. It was as if, for a moment, I had been brushed by the angel's wing.

## 23. A Divinity that Shapes Our Ends

"THERE is a Divinity that shapes our ends, rough hew them as we may." This familiar idea is a part of the folklore of the common life of many peoples. Again and again, we are reminded by the facts of our own lives that there is an aspect of our experience which seems to be beyond our own control and yet which seems ever to manipulate us into position. When such things happen, we call them the work of Fate or Destiny, or some other term which expresses our ignorance of what is at work. The most convenient term is coincidence. But this labeling does not indicate that we have defined any terms; we have merely described a situation or a result.

A classic illustration: Many years ago, the president of a college in Georgia attended a meeting of the International Missionary Alliance in Jerusalem. There he met an Anglican bishop from Uganda who interested him in granting a four-year scholarship for one of his young African friends.

Within two years, the young man set sail from Africa with a round-trip ticket good for four years. From Liverpool he sent a message to the college, announcing the time of arrival in New York, with the request that he be met in order to clear the matter of immigration. It happened the president of the college was ill at the Mayo Clinic in Minnesota. The message was mishandled and nothing was done about it. The young man arrived but there was no one to meet him. The result was, he had to take the next boat back to Liverpool en route home with a broken heart.

Meanwhile, the college president had been discharged from the hospital and on advice of the doctor, decided to take a slow boat to England. In the middle of the Atlantic he decided to walk through Third Class to see if there were any students on board ship. He saw the young African stu-

dent, introduced himself and inquired about his experience
in America. The young man said, "I have been deceived by a
college president who promised my bishop that he would
educate me if my round-trip transportation to America from
Africa could be provided. I tried to reach him but he ignored
my communications and now I go back home in disgrace. The
man's name is Dr. ————." Then Dr. X said, "I am very
sorry. There is a deep misunderstanding. I am Dr. ————."

The young African student took the next boat from Liverpool back to New York. He received his college education,
plus two years of graduate study at Yale, and is now a very
influential person in his own country. One Sunday morning
in March, 1953, he was a visitor at Fellowship Church.

Coincidence—Fate—Providence—Chance—or the Purpose
of God?

## 24. The Experience of Growing Up

ALWAYS the experience of growing up teaches the same lesson:
The hard way of self-reliance—the uneasy tensions of self-
    confidence.
What there is to be done in accordance with the persistent
    desire,
Each must do for himself.
Often by trial and error, by fumblings and blunderings,
Here a little, there a little more,
Step, by uncertain step, we move in the direction of self-
    awareness:

Gathering unto ourselves a personal flavor, a tang of uniqueness.

In this strength of intimate disclosure, each person faces his world,

Does battle with nameless forces,

Conquers and is defeated, wins or loses, waxes strong or weak.

Always experience says, "Rely on your own strength, hold fast to your own resources, desert not your own mind."

In the same sure moment, the same voice whispers, "Upon your own strength, upon your own resource, upon your own mind,

At long last you cannot rely.

Your own strength is weakness

Your own mind is shallow

Your own spirit is feeble."

The paradox:

All experience strips us of much except our sheer strength of mind, of spirit.

All experience reveals that upon these we must not finally depend.

Brooding over us and about us, even in the shadows of the paradox, there is something more—

There is a strength beyond our strength, giving strength to our strength.

Whether we bow our knee before an altar or

Spend our days in the delusions of our significance,

The unalterable picture remains the same;

Sometimes in the stillness of the quiet, if we listen,

We can hear the whisper in the heart
Giving strength to weakness, courage to fear, hope to despair.


## 25. Through the Coming Year

Grant that I may pass through
the coming year with a faithful heart.

THERE will be much to test me and to make weak my strength
before the year ends. In my confusion I shall often say the
word that is not true and do the thing of which I am ashamed.
There will be errors of the mind and great inaccuracies of
judgment which shall render me the victim of my own stu-
pidities. In seeking the light, I shall again and again find
myself walking in darkness. I shall mistake my light for Thy
light and I shall shrink from the responsibility of the choice
I make. All of these things, and more, will be true for me
because I have not yet learned how to keep my hand in Thy
hand.

Nevertheless, grant that I may pass through the coming
year with a faithful heart. May I never give the approval of
my heart to error, to falseness, to weakness, to vainglory, to
sin. Though my days be marked with failures, stumblings,
fallings, let my spirit be free so that Thou mayest take it and
redeem my moments in all the ways my needs reveal. Give
me the quiet assurance of Thy Love and Thy Presence.

Grant that I may pass through
the coming year with a faithful heart.

## 26. The Horns of the Wild Oxen

> From the horns of the wild oxen
> Thou hast answered me.

THE Horns of the Wild Oxen. I recognize the panic and the sharp pain of sheer brutality. Upon each of us there may come the cruel visitation. It may come in the form of a sudden illness, a quick tragedy, or an unexpected loss. It may be a dramatic disappointment, a complete failure or an overwhelming disaster. It may be a radical sense of helplessness in the presence of the sheer agony of a beloved's need or the inspired awareness of a blanket of misery covering the wretchedness of nameless men, women and children. "The horns of the wild oxen," the symbol of unpremeditated destruction from which, at last, none may find sure refuge or adequate protection.

"From the horns of the wild oxen, Thou hast answered me." Here is the Ultimate Protection against final agony. Here is the Steadying Assurance which addresses the central point of the individual's aliveness. Here is the Hand that reaches out to hold and in holding, rescues. Here is the Animated Confidence that undergirds and sustains. In the quietness of this hour, I saturate myself with the spirit of the living God which is THE answer to all the shocks that await me on tomorrow.

> From the horns of the wild oxen
> Thou hast answered me.

# III

## *Life Is Alive*

The awareness that the universe is dynamic gives to the individual the quiet assurance that wherever he may be located he is in immediate candidacy for the strength that comes from a boundless vitality. This fact makes for a universal kinship among all living things. The blessing of self-consciousness makes possible a deliberate relatedness out of which arise all of the joyous overtones of human relations. To understand another human being even dimly is to bring to a point of focus an Infinite Resource. The Psalmist states it by insisting that "the earth is the Lord's and the fullness thereof."

# 1. There is Order in Life

It is a matter of genuine amazement to me that often we are much more willing to grant the fact of mind and deliberation in nature than in matters which have to do with our own lives. In nature we expect order and sense. If we do not find it, we are sure that at some point we have overlooked an important element. Thus we recheck our steps; for always the assumption is present that nature is orderly. This assumption is very important, because it gives meaning to the wide variety of materials which touch our lives from day to day. Fortunately for us, the order which we discover to be in nature becomes the important clue to our understanding of our own bodies and the procedures for keeping them in a state of repair.

And yet many persons who accept without serious question what is stated above, deny that there is any fundamental order in the universe as a whole and certainly in the life of man. They assert that life generally is without meaning except as we play little games of "values" with ourselves. The logic of the position is that order is found everywhere in nature except in the life of the being whose mind discovers that there is order in nature. Curious, isn't it?

The basic reason for this curious attitude is profoundly significant. Wherever there is order, there is responsibility. Something makes for order, something guarantees the order and defines it. This means that at the very center of the orderly process there is deliberateness. Deliberateness means responsibility. When a man assumes that in matters touching his life and the life of man there is no order, only chaos or accident, then he may escape the responsibility for his own actions. If there is order, then there is a basis for value; and if there is value then a man cannot escape relating himself to it. We do not like responsibility. It is much simpler to live as if there were no responsibility for our conscious deeds, as if our unconscious deeds are without moral significance. But deep within us we know that we cannot escape responsibility. Deep within us we know that such an attitude is profoundly false; and that moral cowardice makes us betray our birthright as human beings. The order which we deny in ourselves is forced upon us by the very structure of our bodies and minds. It is this knowledge that is at the basis of the recklessness with which we squander what we would preserve, and destroy what we would give our very lives to hold dear. This is the "body of death" of modern man. Who shall deliver us?

## 2. Unity is in God

THE plaint of the prophet Habakkuk that "the law is slacked and justice never goes forth" has a familiar ring. The lines have an undertone of self-pity which is one of the most natural reactions of those subjected to injustice. The orderly process seems to be ever at the mercy of the disorderly process. Weeds do not have to be cultivated but vegetables must.

Those things in life which make for disintegration seem ever alert, taking advantage of every situation to turn it to their account. The crux of the issue is not merely the fact of wickedness and injustice in life but the supervitality which they always seem to possess. The "evilness" of evil seems to be more dynamic and energizing than the "goodness" of good. When the behavior of the wicked is observed, the intensity of loyalty demanded is indeed striking. There seems to be a general recognition that the stakes are very high and nothing less than a binding devotion will suffice. There is an efficiency, an intelligence about deliberate injustice that yields power even though it may be short-lived. The behavior of the righteous often seems to be weak, indecisive and uncertain. The righteous seem to find it very difficult to make up their minds and to define their terms. The assumption that there is something about goodness that is so inherently superior to evil that it is not necessary to "work" at goodness is thoroughly gratuitous. The notion that the "ground rules" for righteousness and for unrighteousness are the same will not be downed. It is instructive to observe that the same thing that causes strawberries to grow, causes poison ivy to grow, and for exactly the same reasons. When the conditions for growth have been met, then growth follows automatically. The fact that the former is a delight and the latter is a disorder is beside the point. But this is not the whole story. If they are both sustained by the same energies and guaranteed by the same vitality, then it follows that here we are faced with a problem that cuts deeper than the conflict between righteousness and unrighteousness. There must be a unity

deeper than the area of conflict. This unity is in God. Back
of all the outcry against evil, back of all protests, is the
assumption that rejects the ultimate character of evil. This
assumption is present all through the utterances of Habakkuk.
The deep confidence that life will not ultimately sustain evil
is a part of the distilled wisdom of the prophet and the door
of hope through which the generations have passed into the
city of God.

### 3. Shall I be Good?

> Shall I be good because of some reward,
> Because the virtuous act pays dividends?

THE sentence from one of the Naylor sonnets recalls a
familiar aspect of our common experience. It is very difficult
to escape the searching tyranny of Reward and Punishment.
From early childhood we are drilled in the experience of
expecting to be rewarded because we are good and punished
because we are bad. Again and again, to be good means to
us to be approved. If the act is approved by those who rate
highly with us, then it is apt to be regarded as a good act
or a good deed. Under such circumstances, the basis of our
morality is located outside ourselves completely and is resi-
dent in those persons or that person whose esteem we seek
and must have, or we are insecure. It is but a simple step from
this attitude to the one which ascribes the role of Recorder
and Punisher to God. It is most subtle. We may regard ourselves as being free souls, emancipated from superstitions
and even religion, and yet there persists in the background

of our lives the insistent feeling that our ill fortune is
the result of wrong things that we have done. Indeed,
this may be true. There is a wide area of human experience
in which we are involved directly in the category of reaping
and sowing. We cannot escape the logic of this part of the
moral law. Individuals as well as nations do reap what they
sow. But there is more involved in our central question than
this. It is not enough to be good because of some reward,
because the virtuous act pays dividends. The virtuous act may
or may not pay dividends. In the last analysis, men cannot
be persuaded to be good because of the reward either here
or beyond this "vale of tears." Men must finally come to the
place in their maturity which makes them do the good thing
because it *is good*. Not because it is a command, even a divine
command, but because the good deed, the good thought, the
good life is in *itself good*. This is the strength of the good
deed—that it is good. When this is our awareness, then the
whole matter of reward and punishment, approval and dis-
approval, becomes strangely irrelevant.

> Shall I be good because of some reward,
> Because the virtuous act pays dividends?

No! I shall be good because it is *good*.


## 4. Life Abounds

LIFE is its own restraint. There is a profound element of automatic redemption deep within the life process itself. The
magic of healing of the body is but one tremendous example

of the simple fact. The body is a self-healer. All of the doctor's skill is used to release, to activate the healing tendency within the body itself. It is staggering to reflect upon the vast number of attacks that have been made upon the body by all sorts of diseases and the few times that the body succumbs. When there has been illness and the powers of recovery are at work in the body and in the mind, it is thrilling to visualize what must be the process at work. The whole organism seems to be committed to the vast co-operative task of restoration and renewal. Even the conscious mind bends to the task and often one desires to do those things that are a part of the healing design of the body. But we must not be deceived. It is not for us to determine altogether how this "healing design" must operate. Sometimes the timetable is different from the schedule of our demand. And in our rebellion we work against the process. This is important to remember. The crucial point is, that we must put ourselves completely at the disposal of the "will to wholeness," which is an integral part of the plan of life, which is expressive of the God of life. If our spirits are relaxed at their nerve center, we commit ourselves to this will to wholeness and go on living each day with confidence, doing the next thing with quiet enthusiasm. The amazing wonder of it all is, that life abounds in all variety of resources and resourcefulness. Every moment is a divine encounter, every facet is an exposure to the boundless energies by which life is sustained and our spirits made whole. Thus we live joyfully into life and its restraints.

## 5. By Their Fruits

THERE is no escape from the necessity for testing the validity of religious experience or of ethical insight. This insistence finds expression in the folk saying, "The proof of the pudding is in the eating"; or in the biblical injunction, "By their fruits ye shall know them." The mind demands some kind of proof; so does the human spirit. There is always the possibility of self-deception. How do I know that my experience is valid? What evidence is there by which I can test my insight? It is true that I stand in the inside of my own experience, that I know more about it in detail than some observer, however interested he may be. Nevertheless, I must justify my experience in the light of unprejudiced evidence, if such be available; or so it seems. This insistence presupposes that validity of my experience rises or falls upon the degree to which it has a justification beyond the fact itself.

Further, I may not ever be deeply assured that I am not mistaken. I may be appraising my experience in the light of my own great need or of my own previous conditioning or teaching. As a matter of fact, it is true that most of the fundamental decisions which we make are made on the basis of insufficient evidence. We cannot wait for final proof or verification. It would be too late. Thus we wait as long as we can and then act on the basis of the total knowledge up to the present, with the hope that the future may verify our decision. This means that the decision does not have integrity in itself. Its integrity rests upon how it works out, how it unfolds.

It is a very searching insight of religion at its best that its insights and its experience do not rest finally upon any kind of external or experiential validation. The analogy of the good life is relevant. The important thing about the good life is not that it is useful, that it is expedient, that it is practical or the like. These are important, but the supreme thing about the good life is that it is *Good*—Good in and of itself.[1] Thus religion insists that its experience and the ethic it inspires are their own sure integrity. That is why the prophet insists, "Although the fig tree shall not blossom, neither shall fruit be in the vines; the labour of the olive shall fail, and the fields yield no meat; the sheep shall be cut off from the fold, and there shall be no herd in the stalls: Yet I will rejoice in the Lord, I will joy in the God of my salvation."

## 6. The Glad Surprise

THERE is ever something compelling and exhilarating about the glad surprise. The emphasis is upon *glad*. There are surprises that are shocking, startling, frightening and bewildering. But the glad surprise is something different from all of these. It carries with it the element of elation, of life, of something over and beyond the surprise itself. The experience itself comes at many levels: the simple joy that comes when one discovers that the balance in the bank is larger than the personal record indicated—and there is no error in account-

[1] Cf. Number 3, p. 104.

ing; the realization that one does not have his doorkey—the hour is late and everyone is asleep—but someone very thoughtfully left the latch off, "just in case"; the dreaded meeting in a conference to work out some problems of misunderstanding, and things are adjusted without the emotional lacerations anticipated; the report from the doctor's examination that all is well, when one was sure that the physical picture was very serious indeed. All of these surprises are glad!

There is a deeper meaning in the concept of the glad surprise. This meaning has to do with the very ground and foundation of hope about the nature of life itself. The manifestation of this quality in the world about us can best be witnessed in the coming of spring. It is ever a new thing, a glad surprise, the stirring of life at the end of winter. One day there seems to be no sign of life and then almost overnight, swelling buds, delicate blooms, blades of grass, bugs, insects —an entire world of newness everywhere. It is the glad surprise at the end of winter. Often the same experience comes at the end of a long tunnel of tragedy and tribulation. It is as if a man stumbling in the darkness, having lost his way, finds that the spot at which he falls is the foot of a stairway that leads from darkness into light. Such is the glad surprise. This is what Easter means in the experience of the race. This is the resurrection! It is the announcement that life cannot ultimately be conquered by death, that there is no road that is at last swallowed up in an ultimate darkness, that there is strength added when the labors increase, that multiplied peace matches multiplied trials, that life is bottomed by the glad surprise. Take courage, therefore:

> When we have exhausted our store of endurance,
> When our strength has failed ere the day is half done,
> When we reach the end of our hoarded resources,
> Our Father's full giving is only begun.

## 7. Life Goes On

DURING these turbulent times we must remind ourselves repeatedly that life goes on. This we are apt to forget. The wisdom of life transcends our wisdoms; the purpose of life outlasts our purposes; the process of life cushions our processes. The mass attack of disillusion and despair, distilled out of the collapse of hope, has so invaded our thoughts that what we know to be true and valid seems unreal and ephemeral. There seems to be little energy left for aught but futility. This is the great deception. By it whole peoples have gone down to oblivion without the will to affirm the great and permanent strength of the clean and the commonplace. Let us not be deceived. It is just as important as ever to attend to the little graces by which the dignity of our lives is maintained and sustained. Birds still sing; the stars continue to cast their gentle gleam over the desolation of the battlefields, and the heart is still inspired by the kind word and the gracious deed. There is no need to fear evil. There is every need to understand what it does, how it operates in the world, what it draws upon to sustain itself. We must not shrink from the knowledge of the evilness of evil. Over and over we must know that the real target of evil is not destruction of the body, the reduction to rubble of cities; the real target of evil is to corrupt the spirit of man and to give to his soul the contagion of inner disintegration. When this happens, there is nothing left, the very citadel of man is captured and laid waste. Therefore the evil in the world around us must not be allowed to move from without to within. This would be to be overcome by evil. To drink in the beauty that is within reach, to clothe one's life with simple deeds of kindness, to keep alive a sensitiveness to the movement of the spirit of God in the quietness of the human heart and in the workings of the human mind—this is as always the ultimate answer to the great deception.

## 8. Thine is the Power!

How many years ago, we do not know. The setting may have been a simple cell in an ancient monastery. A monk laboriously copied the manuscript of the New Testament. Word by word he copied: "Our Father, which art in heaven, hallowed be Thy name. Thy kingdom come. Thy will be done in earth, as it is in heaven. Give us this day our daily bread. And forgive us our debts, as we forgive our debtors. Lead us not into temptation, but deliver us from evil." Here the prayer ended. The mood of prayer captured the mind and heart of the devout copyist. At long last as if in a trance of exultation, over and over he said it: "For Thine is the kingdom and the

power and the glory . . . forever! AMEN." He may have
written this on the margin of his copy. Later some other
monk, seeing the words in the margin, incorporated them
in the text of the manuscript. The story itself may be imagi-
nary, but the need of exultation which the words depict is
as old as the struggle of the human race for strength to fulfill
the highest dreams and the most lofty longings.

The power—there are many secondary sources for the
power which is of God. There is the power that comes from
the challenge of a great need, deeply felt, in the life of others.
There is a kind of tyranny that human need is capable of
exercising upon us once we are brought into direct contact
with it. In the presence of its imperious demand we are apt
to forget our own limitations, our own inadequacies, even
our own needs. This is one of the reasons why we tend to
reduce our direct exposures to the needs of our fellows. We
know that it will take us out of ourselves, out of our com-
placency and put our resources and ourselves completely at
their disposal. "The note of service must be deepened and
in our care for those who lie wounded or broken along the
road, we shall forget our own wounds and our own weari-
nesses." The need itself seems to create a vacuum pulling into
it with utter ruthlessness that which is capable of ministering
to it. After that kind of experiencing, we are willing to do
in behalf of others what we were incapable of doing without
such a challenge. Once the energy has been released, we
become something more than we were before. A plus is added
to ourselves. And into this added something, we ourselves
have entered. We become, in deeds, the power.

## 9. Make up Your Mind

IT IS often very difficult to make up one's mind. The difficulty may be due to the complexities of the issues involved, or to the limited number of facts available for consideration, or certain fears that overshadow the horizon, or a general habit of indecision that has developed through the years. Sometimes indecision may obtain in small or minor matters, but, in significant matters, the same individual may be forthright, direct and to the point. Or the reverse may be the case. I knew a man who earned his living by capturing native wild animals for a local zoo. He would bring back from the woods rattlesnakes, opossums, coons, alligators and wildcats. All of these he would capture unassisted. He knew no fear. Yet I have seen him break out into a "cold sweat" from sheer panic when his young son approached him with a caterpillar on a leaf. There are people like that in dealing with matters about which they must make up their minds. Of course, one must never forget that postponing a decision may be to decide by default. It is the nearest illusion to think that, if I do not make up my mind, events that are contingent upon me and my decision will await my pleasure. It is true that up to a certain point this may be the case. But eventually the invisible line is passed and my indecision becomes an automatic decision which commits me but which takes the matter out of my hands. The result is often very frustrating indeed. A person likes to feel that he made up his own mind and not that he has been pushed or forced into a decision either by events

or by other persons. It is for this reason that it is most important to develop the ability to make up one's own mind while
there is time. There are some things that can wait indefinitely
and there are others that exhibit varying degrees of urgency.
Much thought and care must be exercised in distinguishing
one from the other. The red sign on the Bay Bridge which
says that, beyond a certain point, there is no stopping or turning, expresses the basic notion here. Always the intimate relation between taking responsibility and making up one's mind
must be held steadily in view.


## 10. Two Areas of Need

THERE are at least two areas of need in which all men are
involved. One is the insistence upon finding something to worship. Everybody has to have something to worship. It is not
optional. It is not merely the result of some particularly significant spiritual bias in personality. There is something native
to the human spirit that insists upon the offering of one's
precious gifts, precious possessions—offering them to something outside of oneself, something that is regarded as su-
premely worthful. What happens when you get a very wonderful piece of good news? What do you do? You want to
tell somebody—somebody who means enough to you to accept
your tidings as a symbol of nearness and devotion. What do
you worship? To what do you bring the most precious incre-
ments of your spirit, your mind and your possessions? The

need is ever present. Whatever it is that holds so central a place in your reaction to living, that is your God!

There is also the need of being a part of the family, the human family, the human race. I am aware that all the race, in some very meaningful sense, breathes through *me*—that I am a part of the very pulsating rhythm of existence. I am not a thing apart, I am not a separate unit; I am deeply involved in the collective experience of aliveness and of human aliveness. If I am cut off so that only my little life breathes through me, only my little hopes course through my mind and spirit, only my little thoughts penetrate my brain, then life for me is not worth living. I must have a sense of deep corporate vitality; nothing less than that will satisfy. Therefore I must manage somehow to keep the lines of communication open between me and the human family. How wonderful it is if I can do this by love, by warmth, by kindling flame of abiding fellowship! Often, if it cannot be done that way, there is resort to hate, to antagonism, to belligerency. The shouting of defiance is the call of my heart for kinship. If a man cannot become the center of an increasing affection, in his desperation he becomes the core of a great rejection. For better or for worse, there is but one family under God and I am a member of it.

## 11. If I Knew You

WILLIAM PENN wrote, "Neither despise, nor oppose, what thou dost not understand." He might have added " 'nor approve' what thou dost not understand." It is very easy to pretend to understand what one does not understand. Often the degree to which we oppose a thing marks the degree to which we do not understand it. Sometimes we use our opposition to an idea to cover up our own ignorance. We express our dislike for things, sometimes for people, when we do not understand the things we pretend to dislike; when we do not know the people for whom we have the antagonism.

> If I knew you and you knew me,
> And each of us could clearly see
> By that inner light divine
> The meaning of your heart and mine;
> I'm sure that we would differ less
> And clasp our hands in friendliness,
> If you knew me, and I knew you.

One has to pay a price for understanding. In the realm of facts, one has to work hard and carefully, weighing and sifting and testing before one arrives at an understanding of them. This takes time as well. There must be a *will* to understand which informs the integrity of one's desire to understand. How much "more true" is it in the understanding of ideas, of experiences, yes, of the complexities of human beings. It takes time and effort and imagination. It does not come merely for the asking. One has to "fool around" the edges of another's life, getting closer and closer to the central place. Where this is lacking, it is easy to cover up one's own lacks by making a negative attitude into a positive appraisal. The basis of one's strength in understanding is the vast and unlimited understanding of God, who is the source and ground of all our being.

## 12. All Life is One

*"They, as part of us, have done this to us."*

IT WAS a very simple statement—"They, as part of us, have done this to us." Think it over very, very carefully. One of the most direct results of a sense of injury is the element of divisiveness or separateness that it introduces immediately. "Look at what they are doing to me!" or "Why do people treat me that way?" It is obvious how this mood, understandable as it is, cuts the tie that binds man to man. Such an attitude establishes a gulf between men, made possible by the effect of their deeds on their own kind. Often we say to ourselves that the only conditions under which it is possible for one person deliberately to injure another is for the injurer to be able to regard himself as being something other than, and perhaps more than, the injured one. There is something utterly fantastic about the thing that takes place in a personality before that personality is able to hurt deliberately. Some kind of immunity against feeling must be established. On the other hand, the injured person seems instinctively to feel that the person who injures him must be different, deeply and profoundly different or else the thing that was done would not have been done. Hence the cry, "Look at what they are doing to me!" But when we begin with the basic idea that all life is one—that there is no such thing as an ultimate detachment of any part of life from the whole—then the meaning of the simple statement, "They, as part of us, have done this to us," begins to make sense. The moment that this is understood, two attitudes become at once apparent. One: it is no longer possible to separate oneself from another person even when that other person behaves as if he were not a part of one's self. What the other person does to me is, in some very real sense, a part of me doing that thing to a part of us. Two: it becomes a reasonable thing for me to hope to understand another person because of the hope that I can and may ultimately understand myself. This is the meaning of the statement, Know thyself, which has been taken more mystically from the statement, "Thou hast seen thy brother, thou hast seen thy God."

## 13. He Prayed for His Friends

IN THE final chapters of the Book of Job there appears a very searching sentence introduced into the drama by the author. The sentence: God turned the captivity of Job when he prayed for his friends. He is suggesting that God was unable to find a resting place in the heart, in the life of Job, until he, Job, altered fundamentally his attitude toward his friends. There seems to be a special rancor reserved for friends when disaffection arises.

It seems simple, sometimes, to deal charitably with those who may be regarded as enemies. There is something rather flattering and condescending about extending grace to one who is beyond the pale. To pray for one's enemies can be a very superior role. But to pray for one's friends—that is another matter. Always there is the implication that one's friends should know better than to behave as they have done. It is hard to forgive one's friends for error in relationships; because each error is regarded as betrayal.

Job's experience is instructive. His friends had come to comfort him, to do the gracious act at a moment of deep distress. He was glad that they remembered him. But when they came, their words were full of judgment. They dealt with Job's predicament, but they did not deal with Job himself. What he needed most desperately was to be understood by them, to be able to place reaction to his tragedy in their responsive hands and find rest. When they were unable to do this for him and with him, he felt betrayed. He was embittered by his experience. Out of his distress, he could understand the Chaldeans who had raided his flocks; he could grasp the helplessness of man in the midst of tantrums of nature which in his case had been destructive of his children. But his friends were in another category. To pray for his friends meant that he had forgiven them. He could not bring them before God unless this relationship was right. It was blasphemous to ask God to do for his friends what Job himself was unwilling to do. When Job was able to pray for his friends, he had solved the basic problem of his suffering and his rebellion. That is why the dramatist says that God turned the captivity of Job when Job prayed for his friends.

## 14. We are All One

LONG AGO, Plotinus wrote, "If we are in unity with the Spirit, we are in unity with each other, and so we are all one." The words of this ancient Greek mystic are suggestive; for they call attention to the underlying unity of all of life. The recognition of the Spirit of God as the unifying principle of all life becomes at once the most crucial experience of man. It says that whoever is aware of the Spirit of God in himself enters the doors that lead into the life of his fellows. The same idea is stated in ethical terms in the New Testament when the suggestion is made that, if a man says he loves God, whom he hath not seen, and does not love his brother who is with him, he is a liar and the truth does not dwell in him. The way is difficult, because it is very comforting to withdraw from the responsibility of unity with one's fellows and to enter alone into the solitary contemplation of God. One can have a perfect orgy of solitary communion without the risks of being misunderstood, of having one's words twisted, of having to be on the defensive about one's true or alleged attitude. In the quiet fellowship with one's God, one may seem to be relieved of any necessity to make headway against heavy odds. This is why one encounters persons of deep piousness and religiosity who are intolerant and actively hostile toward their fellows. Some of the most terrifying hate organizations in the country are made up in large part of persons who are very devout in the worship of their God.

The test to which Plotinus puts us, however, is very searching. To be in unity with the Spirit is to be in unity with one's fellows. Not to be in unity with one's fellows is thereby not to be in unity with the Spirit. The pragmatic test of one's unity with the Spirit is found in the unity with one's fellows. We see what this means when we are involved in the experience of a broken relationship. When I have lost harmony with another, my whole life is thrown out of tune. God tends to be remote and far away when a desert and sea appear between me and another. I draw close to God as I draw close to my fellows. The great incentive remains ever alert; I cannot be at peace without God, and I cannot be truly aware of God if I am not at peace with my fellows. For the sake of my unity with God, I keep working on my relations with my fellows. This is ever the insistence of all ethical religions.

## 15. Man Cannot be Indifferent to Men

"The key to community must be fashioned of a common understanding of life, a common faith, a common commitment." Every person is at long last concerned with community. There is a persistent strain in the human spirit that rejects the experience of isolation as being alien to its genius. It is true that there are moments when the feeling for aloneness, for solitariness, must be honored and respected. Every person has said many times over, "I must get away from it all. I want to be alone." This really means the urgency to catch up with one's self, to clear the bearings, that one's true place in community may be more accurately seen and realized.

But community is the native climate of the human spirit. It is for this reason that we seem most our true selves when we are deeply involved in relations with other selves. Man cannot be indifferent to men. The human race cannot be ignored by the individual man. However skilled a man may be in a particular field of endeavor, however effective he may be in doing a job, there can be no peace of mind until such a man establishes an authentic sense of community with his fellows. He begins always at the primary level. He wants to be related specifically and privately to others. He must share in a common understanding of life with others or another like himself. He must be a part of a common faith with others or another like himself. This is the level at which community begins. It builds outward to include more and more of a man's fellows—but it begins at the primary level. Wherever community at this level is ruptured, some precious part of the self perishes. It is for this reason that the experience of forgiveness, of restoration, plays so crucial a part in the life of every man. It is of the primary relation with individuals that the bridge connecting one to a group or groups is constructed. Always a man is driven to do something about his personal relationships. He must have free and easy access to persons who are immediately significant to him if he is to share deeply in community. This is the very stuff upon which the soul of man feeds; for it is the door through which he enters into the Holy of Holies where God dwells. For behold the dwelling place of God is in the hearts of men! This is the tug of God that pulls each of us to Him. The most direct response is through the *human* heart: my own heart and the hearts of my fellows.

## 16. I Will Not Give Up

IT WAS above the timber line. The steady march of the forest had stopped as if some invisible barrier had been erected beyond which no trees dared move even in single file. Beyond was barrenness, sheer rocks, snow patches and strong untrammeled winds. Here and there were short tufts of evergreen bushes that had somehow managed to survive despite the severe pressures under which they had to live. They were not lush, they lacked the kind of grace of the vegetation below the timber line, but they were alive and hardy. Upon close investigation, however, it was found that these were not ordinary shrubs. The formation of the needles, etc., was identical with that of the trees farther down; as a matter of fact, they looked like branches of the other trees. When one actually examined them, the astounding revelation was that they *were* branches. For, hugging the ground, following the shape of the terrain, were trees that could not grow upright, following the pattern of their kind. Instead, they were growing as vines grow along the ground, and what seemed to be patches of stunted shrubs were rows of branches of growing, developing trees. What must have been the tortuous frustration and the stubborn battle that had finally resulted in this strange phenomenon! It is as if the tree had said, "I am destined to reach for the skies and embrace in my arms the wind, the rain, the snow and the sun, singing my song of joy to all the heavens. But this I cannot do. I have taken root beyond the timber line, and yet I do not want to die; I must not die. I shall make a careful survey of my situation and work out a method, a way of life, that will yield growth and development for me despite the contradictions under which I must eke out my days. In the end I may not look like the other trees, I may not be what all that is within me cries out to be. But I will not give up. I will use to the full every resource in me and about me to answer life with life. In so doing, I shall affirm that this is the kind of universe that sustains, upon demand, the life that is in it." I wonder if I dare to act even as the tree acts. I wonder! I wonder! Do you?

## 17. Take no Thought for Your Life

TAKE no thought. This day I shall desert my anxieties. I shall forsake them—cut them off from the food supply of my spirit. Confident am I that if I do not feed them they cannot long survive. I shall seek to limit my primary exposure to those who exploit my anxieties by their tendency to exaggeration and alarm. I shall seek to broaden my exposure to those whose lives give forth confidence and calmness. Into God's hand do I yield myself this day, with all that it involves for me, with the faith that I can take complete refuge in the knowledge and the love of God. For me this will not be easy, nor do I lightly undertake it.

Take no thought for your life. What a strange thing it is, this injunction! Up to this period of my life, I have seemed to survive by taking thought for my life. Upon deeper reflection, I begin to see that my life is not now, nor has it ever been, my own. I did not create nor have I sustained my life through the years. In so many ways, without my own plans and purposes, hard places have been made soft and rough places smooth. It is a source of immeasurable satisfaction and comfort to me to know that God, who is the Source and Sustainer of life, can be trusted to see me all the way to the end and beyond. Take no thought for your life—it is in God's hands and ever, when I am obeying the laws of life, it is God who works through me.

Take no thought for your life.


## 18. Magic all Around Us

I seek new levels of awareness
of the meaning of the commonplace.

IT IS easy for me to take things for granted and to deal with them without sensitiveness. When have you noticed the color in the sky? When have you looked at the shape and place of a tree? What about the light in the eyes of your friend when he smiles? The gracious manner that your child has in meeting people at the door? The moving insight and the power of the words of a hymn, the music of which you enjoy? The renewal of mind and body after a night of restful sleep? The way the cut in your finger healed, leaving scarcely a trace of the opening? The spontaneous response which overcomes you when you are face to face with some poignant human need? The times when deep within your heart you whisper a thank you to Life, to God or, as you may say, to the Fates!

> There's magic all around us.
> In the rocks and trees, and in the minds of men,
> Deep hidden springs of magic.
> He who strikes the rock *aright,* may find them where he will.[1]

> > I seek new levels of awareness
> > of the meaning of the commonplace.

## 19. The Threads in My Hand

ONLY one end of the threads, I hold in my hand.
The threads go many ways, linking my life with other lives.

One thread comes from a life that is sick; it is taut with anguish
And always there is the lurking fear that the life will snap.
I hold it tenderly. I must not let it go . . .

One thread comes from a high-flying kite;
It quivers with the mighty current of fierce and holy dreaming
Invading the common day with far-off places and visions bright . . .

[1] "Watchers of the Sky," *Watchers of the Sky* by Alfred Noyes. Copyright, 1922, by J. B. Lippincott Company, and used by permission of J. B. Lippincott, Wm. Blackwood & Sons, Ltd., and Alfred Noyes.

One thread comes from the failing hands of an old, old
  friend.
Hardly aware am I of the moment when the tight line slack-
  ened and there was nothing at all—nothing . . .

One thread is but a tangled mass that won't come right;
Mistakes, false starts, lost battles, angry words—a tangled
  mass;
I have tried so hard, but it won't come right . . .

One thread is a strange thread—it is my steadying thread;
When I am lost, I pull it hard and find my way.
When I am saddened, I tighten my grip and gladness glides
  along its quivering path;
When the waste places of my spirit appear in arid confusion,
  the thread becomes a channel of newness of life.

One thread is a strange thread—it is my steadying thread.
God's hand holds the other end . . .

## 20. She Practices Brotherhood

THE telephone rang at seven-fifteen in the morning. And on
the other end was a lady whose voice seemed full of years,
soft but strong. What she had to say was profoundly stirring:
"I am sorry to disturb you so early in the morning, but I
wanted to call you before you left the hotel for the day.
About ten years ago (I am now sixty-nine) I decided to examine my life to see what, if anything, I could do to put into

practice my own convictions about brotherhood. Why I decided this, and not suddenly, I need not say. But I did. The
first thing I discovered was that I knew almost nothing about
other races in my own city, particularly about Negroes. I went
to the library and was given a small list of books and maga-
zines. I began to work. The things I learned! When it seemed
to me that I had my hands on enough facts (and I discovered
you don't need too many facts, because they get in your way),
I plotted a course of action. Then I was stumped. What could
I do? I had no particular abilities, very little energy, and an
extremely modest income. But I did like to talk with people as I met them on the buses and in the stores. I decided that
I would spread the facts I had and my own concern among
all the people whose lives were touched by mine in direct
conversation. It took me some time to develop a simple
approach that would not be an intrusion or a discourtesy. For
several years, I have been doing this on the bus riding into
town each week, in a department store where I have made my
purchases for two decades, and in various other places. Occasionally, I run into a person in the street who stops to intro-
duce himself and to remind me of a previous meeting. One
such person said, 'I guess you have forgotten, but about four
years ago I sat by you on a bus, and I don't know how the
question came up but we talked about the Negroes; and you
started me thinking along lines that had never occurred to
me. You even gave me the name of a book which I noted
and purchased. Since then, I have been instrumental in chang-
ing the whole personnel practice of our business on this question. Thanks to you!' "

Continuing, she said "I know that this is not very much and I guess many people are doing much more. But I thought I would tell you this so that, in your moments of discouragement, you may remember what one simple old lady was doing to help in little ways to right big wrongs. Good-by and God bless you." She did not give me her name, nor her address; she merely shared her testimony and gave her witness.

## 21. A Glory! A Benediction!

SHE sat beside the open hearth, her head tilting to one side as if she were listening for some urgent word. I noticed that this was the first time that I had ever seen her without her hearing aid. There was something white in the right ear, which I mistook for the plastic disc of a new aid to hearing. Closer scrutiny revealed that this was a piece of cotton. It was noticeable also that she was not following the movement of my lips with her customary concentration. And then I knew. For the first time in many years, she was hearing unaided. I gathered in a few brief sentences that she had had an extremely delicate operation on one ear, and that thus far the results had been positive.

"Think of it—to hear the sound of a truck or passing car. I find myself listening to hear the light switch from downstairs. Late at night, I sit in the darkness listening, always listening, to the whole new symphony of sounds beating in upon me. I finger them reverently and gently, distilling from

each new sound the magic of its music and its wonder. What
an exhilaration! What a glory! What a benediction!"

This experience was a high moment among many high
moments of a lifetime. Hearing for me had been a part of the
normal day's experience—a gift of God, the wonder of which
had been dulled long since by the pattern of familiarity. Only
the rare sound, or the unusual combination of sounds had
stood out in my mind. Since then, I have been much more
sensitive to the meanings of sounds. Much I have learned
about the miracle of the moment glorified in a sound, made
up of myriad parts of many melodies. But all of this is threatened constantly by the commonplace—the risk that the glory
will be tamed out by endless repetition. As I left the house
of my friend, my heart whispered many thanks to God, that
through her ears I had heard with new hearing, and sensed
the sheer joy of the Eternal when He created sounds and
grand symphonies of melodies to delight the mind and make
glad the spirit.

## 22. Indebted to a Vast Host

HE WAS a very ordinary-looking man walking along the side-
walk. It was at the close of day but darkness had not yet
begun to spread its mantle everywhere. About three feet from
the curbstone, a group of birds was pecking away at a small
opening in the side of a pink paper bag. They were quarreling
as they pecked because there must have been many sugges-

tions being offered as to the best way to get to the crumbs that were hidden there. The man walked over to the spot; the birds took rapid flight, settling at a respectful distance in the grass, watching. With his foot he turned the bag over, examined it with some care, then reached down and emptied the bag and its contents of bread crumbs. When he had done this, he resumed his walk. As soon as he disappeared, the birds returned to find that a miracle had taken place. Instead of a bag full of hidden crumbs, only a glimpse of which they had seen, there was before them now a full abundance for satisfying their need. The man had gone on his way without even a backward glance. Of course he could have walked away casting his glances back to feast his eyes on the results of his effort. Or he could have withdrawn far enough so as not to disturb the birds, and watched them eat while he congratulated himself because he was kind to birds and extremely sensitive to their needs. But he did none of these things. He went on his way without even a backward glance. Any careful scrutiny of one's own life will reveal the fact that we have been in the predicament of the birds again and again. The thing one needed was somewhat in evidence but out of reach. With all of one's resources, one worked away at the opening, trying first one attack and then another; then some stranger, some unknown writer, some passing comment from another, did the needful thing. We are all of us indebted to a vast host of anonymous persons without whom some necessity would not have been available, some good which came to us, we would have missed. It is not too farfetched to say that living is itself an act of interdependence. However strong we may be or think we are, we are constantly leaning on others. However self-sufficient we are, our strength is always being supplied by others unknown to us whose paths led them down our street or by our house at the moment that we needed the light they could give. We are all of us the birds and we are all of us the man. It is the way of life; it is one of the means by which God activates Himself in the texture of human life and human experience.

## 23. Just a Human Being

HE WAS a tall, very attractive man with a pronounced forehead and a shock of very dark hair. I had met him many years ago. He was blind. From the first, we seemed to be old friends; but I had not gotten acquainted with him in any detailed sense until very recently. When I visited his community, I arranged my schedule so that we could spend several hours together. We talked of many things—books, travel, baseball, and Fellowship Church. And then we talked about blindness, the kind of life a blind man lives and particularly how he regards the fact and the experience of his blindness.

"Since I saw you last," he said, "I have been doing some public speaking, particularly before Service Clubs. It is very difficult for even well-meaning people to regard me as just a human being. Out of sympathy or something, they make it hard for me to keep from feeling sorry for myself. If I do that, I am sunk. A certain sense of humor sometimes saves me. I remember one day being introduced to speak before a club. The chairman urged his group to give me a very courteous hearing because, after all, they were blessed with their eyesight—they were not like me—the least they could do for me was to give me a respectful hearing. It was pretty rugged by the time he was through. When I stood up I took out my handkerchief and simulated tears, saying, 'Please listen to me, please, because I am a poor, helpless, blind man.' Perhaps I should not have done that, but it was in a good clean spirit and to my amazement my take-off was interrupted by a tremendous round of applause from all those present. The point was made.

"One thing I have learned in my blindness. My contact with people is direct and immediate. How a person looks, what he has on, what his gestures convey, not any of the things by which we bolster our self-respect or convey our meanings makes any difference to me. I cannot see—I can only hear. All of your meaning, all of your integrity or looks —it must be put into words. And the words come without clothing. Sometimes it is dreadful—the exposure that is revealed when a person cannot hide behind his customary defenses. Had you thought of it?"

When the time came for me to leave, he walked over to his desk, fumbled through some papers, and came back to my chair. He turned to his wife and asked, "Is this what I think it is, a ten-dollar bill?" "Yes," she replied. Turning to me he said, "I want to give you this for our church. I wish I could do more." He then repeated in measured tones, as to himself—The—Church—for—the—Fellowship—of—*All*—Peoples."

I left his home saying over and over, "God help us to grow up to that meaning and that faith."

## 24. The Growing Edge

LOOK WELL TO THE GROWING EDGE. All around us worlds are dying and new worlds are being born; all around us life is dying and life is being born. The fruit ripens on the tree, the roots are silently at work in the darkness of the earth against a time when there shall be new leaves, fresh blossoms, green fruit. Such is the growing edge! It is the extra breath from the exhausted lung, the one more thing to try when all else has failed, the upward reach of life when weariness closes in upon all endeavor. This is the basis of hope in moments of despair, the incentive to carry on when times are out of joint and men have lost their reason, the source of confidence when worlds crash and dreams whiten into ash. The birth of the child—life's most dramatic answer to death—this is the growing edge incarnate. Look well to the growing edge!

## 25. "No Man is an Island"

"NO MAN is an island, no man lives alone." These words from a poem by John Donne have been set to music and have become the theme of a variety of radio programs which are concerned with aspects of social responsibility. It is of crucial importance for each person to consider how he relates himself to the society of which, of necessity, he is a part. For many people and, at times, for most of us, it is a part of our dreaming to be let alone, to be free of all involvements in the responsibilities of life and for others. This is but natural; often the mood passes. Sometimes we say that our personal load is so heavy that it is all we can do to look after ourselves, with all that that entails. Even as we express such ideas, we are reminded of a wide variety of events that we are never ourselves alone. We are not an island, we do not live alone.

There is no alternative to the insistence that we cannot escape from personal responsibility for the social order in which we live. We are a part of the society in which we function. There can be no health for us if we lose our sense of personal responsibility for the social order. This means that there must be participation in the social process, and that quite specifically. Such participation means the wise and critical use of the ballot; the registering of our intent to share responsibility in government. The moral inference is that there must not be a condemnation of the political process of society if we have been unwilling to stand up and be counted on behalf of the kind of government in which we believe and for which we are willing to work and sacrifice. Where social change seems to be urgent, we must share in that process as responsible, law-abiding citizens. The ethical values by which we live must be implemented on the level of social change. This calls ever for a careful evaluation of the means to which we give our support. The means which we are willing to use must not be in real conflict with the ends which our values inspire. Practically, this means that if we believe in democracy, for instance, we must not be a party to means that make use of bigotry, prejudice and hate. We must search and find the facts that are needed for judgment and cast our lot on the side of the issues which we are willing to embrace as our private and personal ends. In working on behalf of such ends, which are morally right as we see the right, we shall not co-operate with or be a party to means that seem to us evil—means that we would not use in our personal private life. In this sense, we are our brother's keeper; for we will not demand of any man that he do on behalf of society as a whole what as persons we would be loath to do ourselves if we were in his place.

## 26. The Need for Approval

WE CANNOT escape the need for approval. The little child seeks it from mother and father and has a sense of uneasiness and insecurity when it is denied. On behalf of such approval, the child will deny what it knows to be true or say "Yes" to what it knows profoundly to be "No." Later, approval is sought from one's associates, one's friends, one's employer, and so on. We cannot escape the need for approval. It is a searching question: from whom do I seek approval and why?

Why is this person or that person's approval important to me? Why? Why? Why?

It is important to point out that the need for approval is a demand of the personality for establishing a secure basis for self-respect. There is a deep and abiding need for the sense of being related to something that is not ultimately swayed by whim, fancy or mood. There is a boundless hunger far within each one of us for an ultimate sponsorship or guarantor of ourselves. It is only in such assurance can we experience authentic freedom—it is only in such assurance are we released from the tyranny of other minds.

This need of approval that complements the personality, giving to it a sense of well-being and significance, is the very core of the religious assurance. It is here that religion takes on its authenticity and authority in the life of the individual. Stripped of all superficialities, the claim of religion is that the ultimate basis of self-respect, the ultimate guarantor of the life of man, is found in God. To have a sense of being related to Him is the ultimate assurance—to miss this is to miss all. The assurance itself is the meaning of salvation —the lack of the assurance is the meaning of being lost. Hence, the Psalmist says, "If God be for us, *who* can be against us?" The struggle between the individual's assurance, independently arrived at, and the individual's assurance, guaranteed for him and to him by the religious institution, is the essence of the struggle between the church and the mystic. Happy indeed is the man who has made the supreme discovery that there is available to him and in him the living experi-

ence of relatedness to the God of the universe and that in that
relatedness is his hope and the anchor of his security. To miss
this possibility through pride, arrogance, stupidity or indo-
lence is to forfeit the priceless experience of being at peace
whatever may be the storms by which one's life is buffeted
and threatened.

## 27. This is a New Year

THIS is a New Year. The calendar says so. I note the fact by
marking it so when I wish to designate the day and the year
as distinguished from some other day and year. It may be
that my contract says so. It is indicated clearly in the lease
I signed or the agreement I attested. It is curious how much
difference can be marked between two dates—December 31
and January 1.

Yet there are many things that move unchanged, paying no
attention to a device like the calendar or arrangements such
as contracts or leases. There is the habit pattern of an individual life. Changes in that are not noted by the calendar,
even though they may be noted *on* the calendar. Such changes
are noted by events that make for radical shifts in values or
the basic rearrangement of purposes. There are desires of the
heart or moods of the spirit that may flow continuously for
me whatever year the calendar indicates. The lonely heart,
the joyful spirit, the churning anxiety may remain unrelieved,
though the days come and go without end.

But, for many, this will be a New Year. It may mark the

end of relationships of many years' accumulation. It may mean the first encounter with stark tragedy or radical illness or the first quaffing of the cup of bitterness. It may mean the great discovery of the riches of another human heart and the revelation of the secret beauty of one's own. It may mean the beginning of a new kind of living because of marriage, of graduation, of one's first job. It may mean an encounter with God on the lonely road or the hearing of one's name called by Him, high above the noise and din of the surrounding traffic. And when the call is answered, the life becomes invaded by smiling energies never before released, felt or experienced. In whatever sense this year is a New Year for you, may the moment find you eager and unafraid, ready to take it by the hand with joy and with gratitude.

## 28. The Pressure of Crisis

WHEN Lloyd George, the British statesman, was a boy, one of his family responsibilities was to collect firewood for warmth and for cooking. He discovered early that always after a very terrific storm, with high winds and driving rain, he had very little difficulty in finding as much, and more, wood than he needed at the time. When the days were beautiful, sunny and the skies untroubled, firewood was at a premium. Despite the fact that the sunny days were happy ones for him, providing him with long hours to fill his heart with delight, nevertheless, in terms of other needs which were his specific responsibilities, they were his most difficult times. Many years after, he realized what had been happening. During the times of heavy rains and driving winds, many of the dead limbs were broken off and many rotten trees were toppled over. The living things were separated from the dead things. But when the sun was shining and the weather was clear and beautiful, the dead and the not dead were undistinguishable.

The experience of Lloyd George is common to us all. When all is well with our world, there is often no necessity to separate the "dead" from the "not dead" in our lives. Under the pressure of crisis when we need all available vitality, we are apt to discover that much in us is of no account, valueless. When our tree is rocked by mighty winds, all the limbs that do not have free and easy access to what sustains the trunk are torn away; there is nothing to hold them fast.

It is good to know what there is in us that is strong and solidly rooted. It is good to have the assurance that can only come from having ridden the storm and remained intact. Far beside the point is the why of the storm. Beside the point, too, may be the interpretation of the storm that makes of it an active agent of redemption. Given the storm, it is wisdom to know that when it comes, the things that are firmly held by the vitality of the life are apt to remain, chastened but confirmed; while the things that are dead, sterile or lifeless are apt to be torn away. The wheat and tares grow up together but when the time of harvest comes, only wheat is revealed as wheat—and tares remain what they have been all along, tares.

## 29. To Die Unshriven

PERUGINO, the teacher of Raphael, when urged to consult a priest, said dauntlessly, "No, I am curious to see what happens in the next world to me, who dies unshriven." One of my early memories is that of standing by the bedside of a dying relative who, when he was asked whether he was prepared to die, said, "All my life I have been a man. I am not afraid of death; I can face it." In a slightly different key I heard my grandmother say on her ninety-first birthday when an old friend asked her was she ready to die, "Yes, I am ready to die but God has yet to make me *willing*." It is recorded that the father of Clemenceau, a physician, refused extreme unction of the church with the remark that he had lived without such ministry and he could certainly die without it.

The fear of death is often one of the final conquests of the courageous spirit. There are many reasons for this fear. One of the significant ones is the fact that there is something which seems too final and absolute about the separation that death implies. To meet this fear, many things have been contrived by religion and by the imagination of men. There are certain things that are worthy of consideration as we deal with this fateful experience in life. In the first place, it is a universal experience in which all living things share. It confirms the oneness and the solidarity of life. Again, it is a vital part of the life process. In a sense, all of living is a struggle between the will to live and the will to die. Again, there are

some things in life that are worse than death. It is urgent
to remember that death is not the worst thing in the world.
Again, death is an event in life. It is something that occurs
*in* life rather than something that occurs *to* life. The distinction is important and urgently significant. If death is an
event in life, then it must take its place alongside an endless
series of events, none of which exhausts life or determines it.
This is the basis of every fundamental hope about immortality
or what is generally called life after death. The form varies
but the issue is the same. Finally, the glorious thing about
man's encounter with death is the fact that what a man discovers about the meaning of life as he lives it, need not
undergo any change as he meets death. It is a final tribute to
the character of an individual's living if he can die "unshriven" but full-blown as he has lived. Such a man goes
down to his grave with a *shout.*

# IV

## *The Moment of Celebration*

There must always be provision for the ample moment when an event takes on the character of the Sacramental, however such an event may be named in the calendar. The true significance of the event is to be found in the quality of celebration which it inspires in the heart.

## 1. The Season of Remembrance

AGAIN and again, it comes:
The Time of Recollection,
The Season of Remembrance.
Empty vessels of hope fill up again;
Forgotten treasures of dreams reclaim
    their place;
Long-lost memories come trooping back to me.
This is my season of remembrance,
My time of recollection.

Into the challenge of my anguish
I throw the strength of all my hope:
I match the darts of my despair
    with the treasures of my dreams;
Upon the current of my heart
I float the burdens of the years;
I challenge the mind of death
    with my love of life.
Such to me is the Time of Recollection,
The Season of Remembrance.

## 2. Concerning Human Relations

How well do you get along with people? Do they seem to
be glad to see you put in your appearance? Or hadn't you

noticed? Do you make friends easily and lose them the same way? Are you very hard to know? Do you like people or would you rather not be bothered?

To be effective in human relations requires both skill and "feel"; it demands the use of head and heart. There must be understanding as well as desire. Examine the matter of skill, of head, of understanding. There is hardly any substitute for knowledge in human relations. It is crucial to know and understand as much as one can about those with whom one lives, or works, or communes. By this, is not meant something that is negative or derogatory. The meaning has to do with a bill of particulars concerning others—temperament, areas of sensitiveness, handicaps, interests, tastes, disposition, registration of a sense of humor, temper point. All these are partial understandings of the other person. Partial understanding is a snapshot or candid shot of the other person. It is limited, highly circumscribed, but often intensely accurate as far as the instant view is concerned.

Effective human relations require something more. They require a kind of total understanding. This is the area of "feel," of heart, of sensing. The content of total understanding is made up of details of partial understanding, but those details are caught up in a creative synthesis which takes in the quality of intuition. When you say concerning a person, "But that's the way he is"—what is working is your total understanding. It is the total understanding that causes you to be increasingly accurate as to your timing. Have you had the experience of saying something to someone with whom you had a very satisfying relationship and then, even before the sound of your voice disappeared, there was an instant in which you *knew* that you had chosen the wrong time? What you had to say was true, to be sure, but the timing was so bad that the true thing became error before your very eyes. Total understanding tends to alert one as to timing; it enables one to pick up overtones from the other person, which are precious guides in choosing *the* word to say and *the* tone in which to say it. What better plan than to seek to increase one's effectiveness in personal human relations by working at accurate partial understanding in creative combination with total understanding of those for whom one's desires are large or small?

## 3. A Litany of Thanksgiving

TODAY, I make my Sacrament of Thanksgiving.
I begin with the simple things of my days:
    Fresh air to breathe,
    Cool water to drink,
    The taste of food,
    The protection of houses and clothes,
    The comforts of home.
For these, I make an act of Thanksgiving this day!

I bring to mind all the warmth of humankind that I have
    known:
    My mother's arms,
    The strength of my father,

The playmates of my childhood,

The wonderful stories brought to me from the lives of
many who talked of days gone by when fairies and
giants and all kinds of magic held sway:

The tears I have shed, the tears I have seen;

The excitement of laughter and the twinkle in the eye with
its reminder that life is good.

For all these I make an act of Thanksgiving this day.


I finger one by one the messages of hope that awaited me at
the crossroads:

The smile of approval from those who held in their hands the
reins of my security;

The tightening of the grip in a single handshake when I
feared the step before me in the darkness;

The whisper in my heart when the temptation was fiercest and
the claims of appetite were not to be denied;

The crucial word said, the simple sentence from an open page
when my decision hung in the balance.

For all these I make an act of Thanksgiving this day.


I pass before me the mainsprings of my heritage:

The fruits of the labors of countless generations who lived
before me, without whom my own life would have no
meaning;

The seers who saw visions and dreamed dreams;

The prophets who sensed a truth greater than the mind could
grasp and whose words could only find fulfillment in the
years which they would never see;

The workers whose sweat has watered the trees, the leaves of
which are for the healing of the nations;
The pilgrims who set their sails for lands beyond all horizons,
whose courage made paths into new worlds and far-off
places;
The saviors whose blood was shed with a recklessness that
only a dream could inspire and God could command.
For all this I make an act of Thanksgiving this day.

I linger over the meaning of my own life and the commitment
to which I give the loyalty of my heart and mind:
The little purposes in which I have shared with my loves, my
desires, my gifts;
The restlessness which bottoms all I do with its stark insistence that I have never done my best, I have never dared
to reach for the highest;
The big hope that never quite deserts me, that I and my kind
will study war no more, that love and tenderness and all
the inner graces of Almighty affection will cover the life
of the children of God as the waters cover the sea.

All these and more than mind can think and heart can feel,
I make as my sacrament of Thanksgiving to Thee,
Our Father, in humbleness of mind and simplicity of heart.

## 4. Against the Background of the Year

OUR Father, another Christmas has moved within our ken
and our minds linger over many moments that stand stark
against the background of the year—

Moments that filled our cup of fear to the brim, spilling over into the byways of our mind until there was no longer room even to know that we were afraid—

Moments of decision, when all that we were, seemed to hang in the balance, waiting for a gentle nudging of Thy spirit to break the tie and send us on with a new direction, a new desire and new way of life—

Moments of sadness, brought on by the violent collapse or quiet sagging of a lifetime of dream-building upon which our hopes and aspirations rested in sure integrity—

Moments of awareness, when our whole landscape was invaded by the glow of Thy spirit, making dead things come to newness of life and old accepted ways turn into radiant shafts of beauteous light—

Moments of joy mingled with the deadly round of daily living, when all our inward parts clapped their hands and a new song was born in our heart—

Moments of peace amid the noisy clang of many conflicts within and without—

Moments of reassurance, when we discovered that our searching anxieties were groundless, without foundation—

Moments of reconciliation, made possible by a deeper understanding and a greater wisdom—

Moments of renewal, without which life would have been utterly impossible and for us this day there would be no Christmas and no day—

Moments of praise and thanksgiving when, in one grand sweep, the sheer wonder and beauty of living overwhelmed us—

Our Father, another Christmas has moved into our ken and our minds linger over many moments that stand stark against the background of the year.

## 5. "Merry Christmas"

THERE is a strange irony in the usual salutation, "Merry Christmas," when most of the people on this planet are thrown back upon themselves for food which they do not possess, for resources that have long since been exhausted, and for vitality which has already run its course. Despite this condition, the inescapable fact remains that Christmas symbolizes hope even at a moment when hope seems utterly fantastic. The raw materials of the Christmas mood are a newborn baby, a family, friendly animals, and labor. An endless process of births is the perpetual answer of life to the fact of death. It says that life keeps coming on, keeps seeking to fulfill itself, keeps affirming the margin of hope in the presence of desolation, pestilence and despair. It is not an accident that the birth rate seems always to increase during times of war, when the formal processes of man are engaged in the destruction of others. Welling up out of the depths of vast vitality, there is Something at work that is more authentic than the formal, discursive design of the human mind. As long as this is true ultimately, despair about the human race is groundless.

## 6. The Sacrament of Christmas

I MAKE an act of faith toward all mankind,
    Where doubts would linger and suspicions brood.

I make an act of joy toward all sad hearts,
    Where laughter pales and tears abound.

I make an act of strength toward feeble things,
    Where life grows dim and death draws near.

I make an act of trust toward all of life,
    Where fears preside and distrusts keep watch.

I make an act of love toward friend and foe,
    Where trust is weak and hate burns bright.

I make a deed to God of all my days—
    And look out on life with quiet eyes.

## 7. Candles for Christmas

### I Will Light Candles This Christmas

CANDLES of joy despite all sadness,
Candles of hope where despair keeps watch,
Candles of courage for fears ever present,

Candles of peace for tempest-tossed days,
Candles of graces to ease heavy burdens,
Candles of love to inspire all my living,

Candles that will burn all the year long.

## 8. The Season of Affirmation

CHRISTMAS is the season of affirmation.
   I affirm my faith in the little graces of life:
      The urgency of growth, the strength of
         laughter, the vitality of friendship.

   I affirm my confidence in the dignity of man:
      His fortitude in despair, his strength
         in weakness, his love in hatred.

   I affirm my joy in the experience of living:
      The fragrance of nostalgia, the scattered
         moments of delight, the exhilaration of danger.

   I affirm my need of my fellows:
      The offerings of faiths, the gifts of
         variety, the quality of difference.

   I affirm my hunger for God:
      The desire for fulfillment, the ache
         for understanding, the sense of peace.

Christmas is my season of affirmation.

## 9. Gifts on My Altar

I PLACE these gifts on my altar this Christmas;
   Gifts that are mine, as the years are mine:
   The quiet hopes that flood the earnest cargo of my dreams:
   The best of all good things for those I love,
   A fresh new trust for all whose faith is dim.
   The love of life, God's precious gift in reach of all:
   Seeing in each day the seeds of the morrow,
   Finding in each struggle the strength of renewal,
   Seeking in each person the face of my brother.
I place these gifts on my altar this Christmas;
Gifts that are mine, as the years are mine.

## 10. Long Live Life!

THERE is something which seems utterly final about the end
of a year. It means that we are one year older; this is a fact
definite and inexorable. We are twelve months closer to the
end of our physical time span—one year closer to death. It
means that in some important ways we are taken farther
from, or brought closer to, the goal of our living, whatever
that goal may be. It means that some crucial questions which
were unanswered twelve months ago have been finally and
decidedly answered, and whatever doubts there may have
been about the result are completely removed; now, we know.
It means that we are in fuller or lesser possession of ourselves
and our powers than ever before. During the passing of the

twelve months, experiences have come into our lives which revealed certain things about ourselves which we had not suspected. Some new demand was made upon us which caused us to behave in a manner that was stranger to our established pattern of life, and we felt shocked, surprised, enraged or delighted that such was possible for us. We met someone with whom we built the kind of relationship which opened up to us new worlds of wonder and magic, which were completely closed to us a year ago. It means that we are wiser by far than we were at year's beginning. The circling series of events upon whose bosom we have been wafted cut away our pretensions, stripping us bare of much beneath which we have hidden even from ourselves; when we saw ourselves revealed, there was born a wisdom about life and its meaning that makes us say with all our hearts, this day, that life is good, not evil. It means that we have been able to watch, as if bewitched, while the illumined finger of God pointed out a path through the surrounding darkness where no path lay; exposed to our surprised gaze a door where we were sure there was only a blank wall; revealed the strong arms and assuring voices of friends when we were sure that in our plight we were alone, utterly and starkly alone. All of these meanings and many more counsel us that because life is dynamic and we are deeply alive, the end of the year can mean only the end of the year, not the end of life, not the end of us, not even the end of time. We turn our faces toward the year being born with a riding hope that will carry us into the days ahead with courage and with confidence. The old year dies; the new year is being born— Long live Life!

## 11. Blessings at Year's End

I REMEMBER with gratitude the fruits of the labors of others, which I have shared as a part of the normal experience of daily living.

I remember the beautiful things that I have seen, heard and felt—some, as a result of definite seeking on my part, and many that came unheralded into my path, warming my heart and rejoicing my spirit.

I remember the moments of distress that proved to be groundless and those that taught me profoundly about the evilness of evil and the goodness of good.

I remember the new people I have met, from whom I have caught glimpses of the meaning of my own life and the true character of human dignity.

I remember the dreams that haunted me during the year, keeping me ever mindful of goals and hopes which I did not realize but from which I drew inspiration to sustain my life and keep steady my purposes.

I remember the awareness of the spirit of God that sought me out in my aloneness and gave to me a sense of assurance that undercut my despair and confirmed my life with new courage and abiding hope.

# V

## *Meditations of the Heart*

"Let the words of my mouth and the meditation of my heart be acceptable in Thy sight."

## 1. Thy Light Within Me

*Kindle Thy light within me, O God!*

KINDLE Thy light within me, that all my darkness may be clearly defined. It is so easy for me to recognize and respond to the darkness in others. Far more conscious am I of the error of others than of my own. The temptation is ever present to compare my strengths with another's weaknesses— to my own advantage, to my own self-glory. Searchingly, there wells up in my mind the terrible thought: "I thank thee that I am not as other men."

Kindle Thy light within me, O God, that I may be guarded against self-deception and the vanity that creeps into my spirit where a shadow is cast between me and Thy scrutiny. I must know through all the reaches of my spirit that my light at its best is dim and clouded with shadow! Teach me the technique by which I can lay bare not merely my failures, my shortcomings, my sin; but also my successes, my strengths and my righteousness.

Kindle Thy light within me, O God, that Thy glow may be spread over all of my life; yea indeed, that Thy glow may be spread over all of my life. More and more, may Thy light give radiance to my flickering candle, fresh vigor to my struggling intent, and renewal to my flagging spirit. Without Thy light within me, I must spend my years fumbling in my darkness.

Kindle Thy light within me, O God!


## 2. "I Will Lift up Mine Eyes"

I WILL lift up mine eyes. Scarcely knowing it, I have become increasingly self-centered, my mind focused upon all the details of my little life and the endless trivialities of a daily routine. I hover over all my little aches and pains, my petty annoyances, my little frustrations, while the band around my head tightens and tightens until at last I would despair completely . . . Then out of no place comes sometimes a gentle, sometimes startling, reminder and I lift up mine eyes. The reminder may be a tale of heroism and courage brought to me over the sound waves of the air; it may be the snatches of a melody long ago forgotten, but with it come flooding in vast recollections of other days freighted with beauty and tenderness; it may be a chance telephone call that nets a reassurance that what I can do for someone beyond the borders of my place relates me to him so urgently that my self-indulgence shames my spirit and chastises my mind.

I will lift up mine eyes. I will lift up mine eyes to life, that I may read the guideposts along my way and not miss the important turning in the road. I will lift up mine eyes to love, that I may not close the door of my heart to the knocking hand, the tender cry, the anxious reach. I will lift up mine eyes to God, that I may meet His spirit not only in the high place, the great moment, the penetrating call, but also in the byways, the little duties, the stinging irritations and the sad and bottomless renunciations. And for me this is enough.

## 3. Abundance of Faith

*I have faith; help Thou my lack!*

I HAVE faith. I live by my faith even as all men do: faith in this day, that it will blend into tomorrow; faith in my mind, that understandings may be reliable; faith in my heart, that feelings may be trustworthy; faith in my friends, that we may joy one another's hours; faith in the world, that I may not fail it; faith in life, that all my ventures may be bottomed; faith in God, that my hope may not perish. I have faith.

I have faith; help Thou my lack. My faith in this day makes clear my lack of it. Faith in my own mind delivers me to error. Faith in my own heart reveals my blindness. Faith in my friends reveals my unworthiness. Faith in the world points up my own failures. Faith in God defines me as sinner. I have faith; help Thou my lack of it.

Because no man can desire what he does not already possess and no man can want what he is not already sharing, I seek with all my heart an abundance of faith, that my lack may be redeemed and my faith may be full.

## 4. How Wonderful!

*I lay bare before God my enthusiasms.*

How wonderful it is to be able to feel things deeply!

The sheer delight of fresh air when you have been indoors all day;

The never ending wonder of sunrise and sunset;

The sound of wind through the trees and the utter wetness of the rain;

The exictement of finding something that was lost and is found:

My fountain pen,

A beautiful word forgotten,

The return of an old book,

The reconciliation after estrangement,

The first step after months of illness.

How moving is the sheer wonder of being necessary to the life of another!

The source of food for a dog, a cat;

The giving of a gentle word when you did not know that such a word was desperately needed;

The sharing of so little at the crucial point of acute urgency;

The invasion of the mind and heart with a sense of Presence in which all of one's being suddenly becomes God's dwelling place.

*I lay bare before God my enthusiasms this day.*

## 5. I Surrender to God

*To God I make a full surrender.*

I SURRENDER to God the nerve center of my consent. This is the very core of my will, the mainspring of my desiring, the essence of my conscious thought.

I surrender to God the outlying districts of my self. These are the side streets down which I walk at night, the alleys of my desires, the parts of me that have not been laid out with streets, the wooded area, the swamps and marshlands of my character.

I surrender to God the things in my world to which I am related. These are the work I do, the things I own or that threaten me with their ownership, the points at which I carry social responsibility among my fellows, the money I earn, my delight in clothes and good food.

I surrender to God the hopes, dreams and desires of my heart. These are the things I reserve for my innermost communion; these are the fires that burn on the various altars of my life; these are the outreaches of my spirit enveloping all the hurt, the pain, the injustices and the cruelties of life. These are the things by which I live and carry on.

*To God I make a full surrender this day.*

## 6. To Overcome Evil

I seek the strength to overcome evil.

I SEEK the strength to overcome the tendency to evil in my own heart.

I recognize the tendency to do the unkind thing when the mood of retaliation or revenge rides high in my spirit;

I recognize the tendency to make of others a means to my own ends;

I recognize the tendency to yield to fear and cowardice when fearlessness and courage seem to fit easily into the pattern of my security.

I seek the strength to overcome the tendency to evil in my own heart.

I seek the strength to overcome the evil that is present all about me.

I recognize the evil in much of the organized life about me;

I recognize the evil in the will to power as found in groups, institutions and individuals;

I recognize the terrible havoc of hate and bitterness which makes for fear and panic in the common life.

I seek the strength to overcome the evil that is present all about me.

I seek the strength to overcome evil; I must not be overcome by evil.

I seek the purification of my own heart, the purging of my
   own motives;
I seek the strength to withstand the logic of bitterness, the
   terrible divisiveness of hate, the demonic triumph of the
   conquest of others.

What I seek for myself I desire with all my heart for friend
   and foe alike.

I seek the strength to overcome evil.

## 7. More Holy!

Lord, I want to be more holy.

LORD, I want to be more holy in my mind. My thoughts tend
ever to be divisive and scattered. In so many ways, my mind
is a house divided; and the conflicts rage up and down all my
corridors. I need wholeness. Oh, that my mind may be stilled
by Thy holy hush! Lord, I want to be more holy in my mind.

Lord, I want to be more holy in my words. Words are my
common tools of communication. All that many know of
me are the words used as connecting links between my inward
parts and theirs. The temptation is ever to use words as in-
struments of confusion and disorder. Words can sting, enrage,
humiliate. Words! oh, that Thy holy quiet may invade my
words, that they may heal, bless and make whole bruised,
broken and fearful ones!

Lord, I want to be more holy in my heart. Here is the citadel
of all my desiring, where my hopes are born and all the deep
resolutions of my spirit take wings. In this center, my fears
are nourished and all my hates are nurtured. Here my loves
are cherished and all the deep hungers of my spirit are honored without quivering and without shock. In my heart above
all else, let Thy love and integrity envelop me until my love
is perfected and the last vestige of my desiring is no longer
in conflict with Thy spirit. Lord, I want to be more holy in
my heart.

Lord, I want to be more holy.

## 8. To See and to Do

I SEEK courage to see the true thing. It is a fearful admission
that courage is required to see the true thing. So much of my
vision is blurred by my fears, my anxieties, my narrow self-
interests that I find difficulty sometimes in giving full range
to a searching scrutiny. It may be that I suspect the effect on
me of seeing things in their true light. Waiting in the quiet
experience of worship I seek the courage, the push of God, to
see the true thing in everything with which I am involved.

I seek courage to do the true thing. To *see* the true thing is
not necessarily to *do* the true thing. It may be that it takes a
heightened form of courage to do the true thing. The act
carries with it its own commitment. The act of a person finally
involves the person and he is required at last to back his deed.
Therefore, to do the true thing places a searching liability

on the integrity of the person who does the deed. We want always to escape the full liability for the deed. The truer the deed, the more the responsibility involves all of a man's life. I seek courage to do the true thing that my own life may not be double talk. Here, in the quietness of worshipful waiting, I seek courage to do the true thing.

I seek courage to see and to do the true thing.


## 9. "They That Wait Upon the Lord . . ."

THEY that wait upon the Lord shall renew their strength.

How hard it is to wait for the renewal of my strength. I know that I am surrounded by all kinds of limitations of mind and spirit—even of will. I want to wait upon the Lord but somehow I cannot bring myself to it. For so long, I have depended upon my own efforts that I must be taught trust even as a little child knows trust. This is a discipline. And yet it does not have the elements of discipline in it. Discipline means effort at times, self-control, a certain mastery of self, or of the situation. But the discipline of trust is a putting down, an easing up, a releasing of tension, an intense relaxation of spirit. Somehow this release is identified in my mind with failure, with weakness of which something within me is afraid and ashamed.

Teach me, O God, the simple lesson of trust.

Bring into my sorely pressed spirit the *sure confidence* of birds floating in the sky with nothing to support them but the automatic trust of wings; or the *sure confidence* of fish that keeps them from drowning with nothing to save but the automatic use of their gills. Teach me to trust, to work for the renewal of my strength; all without pressure, without paying hostage to my anxieties.

> "They that wait upon the Lord
> shall renew their strength."

## 10. More Loving in My Heart

"I want to be more loving in my heart!"

I WANT to be more loving. Often there are good and sufficient reasons for exercising what seems a clean direct resentment. Again and again, I find it hard to hold in check the sharp retort, the biting comeback when it seems that someone has done violence to my self-respect and decent regard. How natural it seems to "give as good as I get," to "take nothing lying down," to announce to all and sundry in a thousand ways that "no one can run over me and get away with it!" All this is a part of the thicket in which my heart gets caught again and again. Deep within me, I want to be more loving— to glow with a warmth that will take the chill off the room which I share with those whose lives touch mine in the traffic of my goings and comings. I want to be more loving!

I want to be more loving in my heart! It is often easy to have the idea in mind, the plan to be more loving. To see it with my mind and give assent to the thought of being loving

—this is crystal clear. But I want to be more loving in my heart! I must feel like loving; I must ease the tension in my heart that ejects the sharp barb, the stinging word. I want to be more loving in my heart that, with unconscious awareness and deliberate intent, I shall be a kind, a gracious human being. Thus, those who walk the way with me may find it easier to love, to be gracious because of the Love of God which is increasingly expressed in my living.

"I want to be more loving in my heart!"

## 11. Teach Me Thy Grace

TEACH me Thy Grace in all the little things of life.

My days are surrounded by myriad little things. There are the little words of every day: simple greetings, yes and no, commonplace expressions of courtesy, minor services of daily routine. There are many little tastes: bread, milk, tea, coffee, salt, sugar, meat, all blended to satisfy hunger and to meet bodily demand. There are little deeds of unasked-for kindness: a button sewed on, a shared personal delight, a gentle reminder of something that had slipped out of mind. Teach me Thy Grace in all the little things of life.

Teach me Thy Grace in the daily work by which I earn my keep and the keep of those dependent upon me.

There are duties demanded of me that irk and irritate, dulling the cutting edge of joy in labor. There is the fatigue that burrows deep into the citadel of my sense of well-being, rendering me brittle, sharp in speech, and short in patience. There is the pride, the arrogance that comes when I turn my eyes from the high level of my intent and look coldly at the lesser deeds of some who walk the way with me. There is the tendency to wrap myself in garments of my own compassion ending in the muck of self-pity and unhealthy moodiness.

Teach me Thy Grace in the daily work by which I earn my keep and the keep of those dependent upon me.

Teach me Thy Grace.

## 12. A Gracious Spirit

I seek this day a gracious spirit.

I SEEK a gracious spirit in dealing with my own conflicts. It is often easy for me to be extremely hard on myself. Often I tend to give myself the disadvantage and to wallow in blame and condemnation as distinguished from self-pity. It is a part of my pretense to be gracious in my spirit in dealing with conflicts at the point in which others are involved, but not with myself. Is this really true, or is it just the reverse? Do I dare expose all of my intent to the scrutiny of God? Dare I seek the understanding of God and His wisdom in facing my own conflict? Again and again, I am aware that the Light not only illumines but it also *burns*.

I seek a gracious spirit in dealing with the injustices of the would. This I do not confuse with softness, or fear, or cowardice, or sentimentality. I must know clearly the evilness of evil and recognize it for what it is—stark, brutal, terrifying. I must oppose it, place the full weight of whatever forces I have thoroughly against it. At the same time, I cannot escape the fact that every judgment is a self-judgment, that even as I resist evil I share the guilt of evil. It is this sense of sharing the guilt of evil that should inspire the gracious spirit in dealing with injustice. I do not want to admit even before God the necessity for this spirit. I fear that it will make me soft and weak. It is out of the depths of my own imperfections that I dare seek the gracious spirit as I wait in the presence of God this day.

*I seek this day a gracious spirit.*


## 13. I Seek Renewal

*I seek the renewal of the spirit of my mind.*

THERE is a spirit of mind without which it is impossible to discern truth. It is this set of mind that makes possible the experience of truth and distinguishes it from the experience of error. It is this spirit that recognizes or senses the false, the dishonest, the bogus thing. It is this attitude that determines the use to which facts are put.

This spirit of mind works in our behavior, in what we do, in what we say, whether our acts are strictly moral in character, or whether they have to do with the manner in which we deal with each other or the traffic of the market place or aught else. This spirit of mind is the factor upon which the integrity of performance rests.

Constantly, I must seek the renewal of the spirit of my mind, lest I become insensitive, dulled, unresponsive to the creative movement of the spirit of God with which life is instinct. True, the spirit of my mind is a gift from God but it must be ever held before Him for testing, for squaring.

Here in the quietness I seek the renewal of the spirit of my mind that I may be a living, vital instrument in His hands, this day!

> I seek the renewal of the spirit of my mind.


## 14. "Still Dews of Quietness"

> "Drop Thy still dews of quietness
> Till all our strivings cease."

"Drop Thy still dews of quietness." "Still dews of quietness" is a happy phrase which suggests a mood, an atmosphere, rather than an idea or a concept. It is a feeling tone of peace, of tranquillity, that settles down over one's spirit. It is the thing that can happen only when one somehow manages to "stay put" for a spell. How wonderful to sit alone, with one's own life parts gathered together, and sense the whole of one's interior landscape's being invaded by a blanket of calm—by the still dews of quietness. This I must cultivate more and more and with ever greater frequency.

"Till all our strivings cease." How deep and often bitter are the strivings within me! The conflicts of indecision, the conflicts of loyalty, the struggle between good and evil courses of conduct, all this and much more makes of my spirit a battleground, a citadel of tempests raging. All of this is a part of me; all of this must be stilled—must be settled. Oh, how my soul cries out for moments when the battle does not rage, when I hear the whisper of the still small voice giving me reassurance and renewal. After which I can go forward without fear but with confidence that the way I take is *The Way* for me.

> "Drop Thy still dews of quietness
> Till all our strivings cease."

## 15. The Outer Life and the Inward Sanctuary

> I determine to live the outer life
> in the inward sanctuary.

OFTEN it is very hard for me to realize that I am one. The outer life seems utterly outer. It seems a part of a separate order. It is made up of the things I do, of my relationship of one kind or another with work, play, job, people and things. The standard by which the outer is judged tends to be an artificial standard, made up of that which is convenient, practical, expedient. The outer seems public, it seems ever to be an external net of physical relationships.

The inward sanctuary is my sanctuary. It is the place

where I keep my trust with all my meanings and my values. It is the quiet place where the ultimate issues of my life are determined. What I know of myself, my meaning; what I know of God, His meaning; all this, and much more, is made clear in my secret place. It seems strangely incongruous, often, to bring into my secret place the rasping, gritty noises of my outer life. Again, this may be for me merely an alibi. For I know that in the searching light of my inward sanctuary all the faults, limitations and evil of my outer life stand clearly revealed for what they are.

I determine to live the outer life in the inward sanctuary. The outer life must find its meaning, the source of its strength in the inward sanctuary. As this is done, the gulf between outer and inner will narrow and my life will be increasingly whole and of one piece. What I do in the outer will be blessed by the holiness of the inward sanctuary; for indeed it shall all be one.

## 16. I Surrender Myself to God

THE central element in communion with God is the act of self-surrender. The symbol of my prayer this day is the open heart. It is most natural for me to think of prayer in terms of the open hand. My needs are so great and often so desperate that there seems to be naught besides my own urgency. I must open my heart to God. This will include my own deep urgencies and all the warp and woof of my desiring. These things, deep within, I must trust with the full awareness that more important even than self-realization is the true glorify-ing of God. Somehow I must make God central to me and in me, over and above the use to which I wish or need to put His energy and His power.

I surrender myself to God without any conditions or reser-vations. I shall not bargain with Him. I shall not make my surrender piecemeal but I shall lay bare the very center of me, that all of my very being shall be charged with the creative energy of God. Little by little, or vast area by vast area, my life must be transmuted in the life of God. As this happens, I come into the meaning of true freedom and the burdens that I seemed unable to bear are floated in the current of the life and love of God.

The central element in communion with God is the act of self-surrender.

## 17. God Seeks Me

### God is seeking me this moment.

AGAIN and again I am conscious that I am seeking God. There is ever present in me a searching longing for some ultimate resting place for my spirit—some final haven of refuge from storms and upheavals of life. I seek ever the kind of peace that can pervade my total life, finding its quiet way into all the hidden crevices of my being and covering me completely with a vast tranquillity. This I seek not because

I am a coward, not because I am afraid of life or of living, but because the urge seems to steady me to the very core.

With sustained excitement, I recall what, in my own urgency, I had forgotten: God is seeking me. Blessed remembrance! God is seeking me. Wonderful assurance. God is seeking me. This is the meaning of my longing, this is the warp of my desiring, this is my point. The searching that keeps the sand hot under my feet is but my response to His seeking. Therefore, this moment, I will be still, I will quiet my reaching out, I will abide; for to know really that God is seeking me; to be aware of that NOW is to be found of Him. Then, as if by a miracle, He becomes the answer to my need. It sufficeth now and forever that *I am* found of Him.

God is seeking me this moment.

## 18. Not We Ourselves

It is God who hath made us<br>and not we ourselves.

IN MANY ways we act as if we ourselves are the creators of life and of our own lives in particular. How much strength, how much power do I have, actually? What is it that, of my own self, I can achieve? How many of my thoughts are *my* thoughts? I wonder. With reference to what may I honestly say, "I did it"? And yet there is ever the claim: this is my life, this is my deed, this thought is my thought. Always the ego shouts aloud its defiance in strident (or muted) tones. Somehow I must reduce my self-centeredness, I must scale down my ego-bump. Somehow I must relate myself to something more than I am, more than I can be when I am completely and thoroughly expressed.

I must know clearly that it is God who is the Author and Creator of my life. This is why, in the light of this reference, my own little life finds its proper place and meaning. This is the secret of humility—I cannot be humble unless I have truly found something about which I *must* be humble. There can be no health in me, nothing but a sickening arrogance and stalking pride until my relation to God scales me down to size. Without that experience, I am unbearable to my friends and a burden to myself. This I must say and in its light order my ways and direct my path. This I remember to do as I wait in the silence of this hour.

> It is God who hath made us
> and not we ourselves.

## 19. Many Assurances of Faith

> The Lord shall keep my going out and my coming in.

THE assurances of faith are many:

My faith in myself keeps me from overestimating or underestimating my own powers. It guards me against the pitfall of depression over personal failures or arrogance over personal triumphs. It centers my spirit upon that in me which is authentic and genuine and keeps me from betraying my own soul. My faith in my fellows keeps me from confusing compassion with pity, sympathy with sentimentality, love with emotional reaction. It slows down the swiftness of my judgment of my fellows and urges me to wait out all disaffection. It keeps the way open for free and often easy access to my fellows and of my fellows to me.

My faith in life teaches me that life is its own restraint, that life can be depended upon to float on its bosom all calamities, all tragedies, all disorders. It leads me directly to the source of life which is at once the goal of life—God. It feeds the springs of my courage and breaks the wall of isolation that sometimes shuts me in; and I am no longer afraid.

The Lord shall keep my going out and my coming in.

## 20. The Wisdom of Patience

God grant me the wisdom of patience.

GOD grant me the wisdom of patience. Let me see clearly this day the difference between patience and cowardice, between patience and fear, between patience and weakness. At my moments of confusion, give me the insight needful for Thy purpose in me. Teach me that my fear of impatience may be a mere indulgence. There are some things in the presence of which I dare not be patient lest they destroy and render evil even the good intent and the holy will. God grant me the wisdom of patience.

The wisdom of patience I seek this day. Patience in understanding myself and dealing with me. Let me so understand the tendencies of my own spirit, the true motives that ride at my masthead, that I am more and more willing to work out my own solutions with confidence and courage. Patience to see and understand, this I seek today. At many points, I am a disappointment to myself: my interests are high and good, my purposes are keyed to the increasing of meaning and enrichment of all life; and yet I fumble and make for confusion and chaos. Even the words I speak at times convey a spirit of ill that I did not know I possessed and certainly did not mean. In my disgust over my own failure, I lose patience with myself and bog down in irritation and frustration. At such times, even now, teach me the wisdom of patience to work with myself, seeking whatever help is needful to the end that I may be whole and undivided in Thy sight.

God grant me the wisdom of patience.

## 21. The Crucial Issues

Teach me to affirm life this day!

TEACH me to affirm life. Always I am making decisions. There are some decisions that are deliberately negative. They cut across everything in me that is positive and affirming. They may involve much or little as far as my immediate destiny is concerned.

It is a crucial thing to come to a point of decision, to weigh courses of action, to sense the meaning of directions. It is in such a moment that a man knows whether he is on the side of life or of death, and the choice is his to make. To affirm life is to accept growth, to accept challenge, to move with all of one's full-orbed intent in response to the deepest that stirs within. Then the miracle takes place; the deepest thing in man somehow makes contact with the deepest thing in life, and he knows that the decision is right—that the decision is on the side of life and not death. Of course, it may be difficult, it may cause much headache and disturbance of a kind, even upheaval, but the issue is never in doubt. It is a terrible thing to make a decision which a man knows, somewhere in the profound recesses of his spirit, is against life. Something dies within; and from that death where can rebirth be found?

Our Father, in whose hands abides the ultimate destiny of Thy children, be with us, stir actively within us, when we are face to face with the crucial issues of our spirits. Teach us to overcome our fear of life; and in that freedom may we learn to understand life and, in our understanding of life, to love life. Steady us that we may cast our vote for and not against life. Teach us to affirm life—this moment!

## 22. When Life Grows Dingy

I ACKNOWLEDGE the commonplace in my life and my surroundings.

I have been letting life grow dingy on my sleeve. Often

it is very easy to take all things for granted. This I do with my friends; often also with the joys that are inherent in much of my living; also with the blessings and graces of life without which much of living would be utterly beyond the springs of my endurance. I acknowledge the commonplace in my life and my surroundings.

I seek this day an active wonder.

An active wonder is the desperate need of my mind and spirit. The awareness of the unexplored and the untried until I find my way into their secret places, this I need and I seek. The illumination of wonder over my familiar landscape, revealing in ordinary things, fresh glories; making manifest in my familiar heights and depths that which I have never known—this I need and *I seek* this day. Teach me this day to expose to Thy scrutiny, my Father, the frayed edges of my aliveness until they are renewed and freshened by Thy Healing and Thy Love.


## 23. We Yield to the Love of God

WE BARE our lives to the scrutiny, to the judgment, to the love of God. There is so much that burdens the mind, that peoples the thoughts, that again and again we are confused even in the great quiet Presence of God.

We yield to Him our confusions: the chaos of our minds and spirits; the tensions that tame the glory of the love of God out of our lives.

We yield to Him our frailties and our limitations: our quiet physical pains and the long chain of anxieties they inspire; the fatigue of spirit, because with reference to our private burdens often we become so tired.

We yield the desires of our minds and hearts: the private intimate wishes by which again and again the springs of our activities are fed and kept alive.

We yield the desires of which we are ashamed: those desires that buffet our spirits and torture our minds and yet seem to cling to us with such tenacity.

We yield our joys: the joy in being alive; the joy in renewed friendships; the joy in re-established and reconciled lives; the joy in the day's work and the night's rest; the sheer joy of being loved, of caring and being cared for.

We yield our concerns for the world where we are exposed to much that casts down and depresses, to little that uplifts and inspires: war and the threat of war; the long loneliness and the deathwatch which seems to stalk our culture and fill our civilization with deadly dry rot.

We yield our lives, the nerve centers of our consent: lest the mainsprings of all our values collapse and we become like shadows in the night.

All of this—and more than tongue can say and heart can feel and mind can think—all of this we yield to the scrutiny, to the judgment, to the love of God.

## 24. The Humble Spirit

The humble spirit and the contrite heart
Thou givest to him who seekest with true devotion.

THE humble spirit. I learn the meaning of the humble spirit
from the earth. The earth takes into itself the rain, the heat
of the sun, and it works with these gifts of life to bring the
magic out of itself to be used for growth and sustenance of
all living things. The earth is good because it takes what life
gives, and within itself it uses its gifts to make life abound.
It waits for fruition and gathers its fruit unto itself for more
life and more growing. I shall learn of the earth the meaning
of the humble spirit.

The contrite heart. I will yield all the hard places of my heart
to the softening influence of the Spirit of God. Despite my
pride, my pain and my vainglory, I will yield every stubborn
bit of the cancerous growth in my heart to God until He
makes my heart whole, one united outlet of His spirit. It will
not be easy, not simple perhaps, but here in the quietness I
give up to Him all the lumps, the unresolved bits of me.

The humble spirit and the contrite heart
Thou givest to him who seekest with true devotion.

## 25. Life Without Cares

Cast all your care upon God; for He careth for you.

A LIFE without cares! Such is frequently the burden of the heart's desiring. There is no one who has not felt the emptiness of exhaustion, the dead weight of burdens greater than can be carried, the utter panic shooting through one's total being as the heavy load settles into place. All this is a familiar part of living experience. The urge to escape—the hunger to be let alone for a span, however brief—is also a familiar part of living experience.

Who has not looked upon his own life with varying degrees of resentment, sensed sometimes clearly, and rebelliously uttered at other times? It may be some physical handicap that slows one up in the general race; it may be some scar of the mind that mars the wholeness and beauty of the spirit; it may be the backwash, the residue, of some ghastly error made in a moment when all of life was caught in the frightful grip of a decision of the moment; and now there is no choice but to abide by it, days without end.

Who has not stood beside the tragedy of a loved one and been paralyzed by the sheer impotence and helplessness of love, even, to redeem and restore? Something surely can be done, but what? There must be help available, but where? There has to be an answer, but how to find it?

The Word from the Book is: "Cast all your care upon God, for He careth for you." This is no idle word—no mere utterance of piety nestled in a great fear. This is the word of courage and of faith. It is the assertion of the Spirit in man calling man to act in the light of his true heritage. Try it today with reference to something definite and concrete. What a difference! This day will become a new day among all the days of your life.

## 26. The Valley of Death

Though I walk through the Valley of the Shadow of Death,
I will fear no evil.

"THOUGH I walk through the Valley of the Shadow." My journey through the Valley of the Shadow of Death may be hurried, swift. If so, this fact may reduce my fear, my anxiety. The time interval may be so short, and so much may happen, that fear does not have a chance at me. This lack of fear occurs with acute illness sometimes or with exposure to sudden danger. But if the illness is long drawn out and there is time for the gradual unfolding of the real meaning of my condition, then I seem to be more completely at the disposal of all kinds of fears as well as of fear itself. Thus I *walk* through the Valley of the Shadow.

"The Valley of the Shadow of Death." Is there some important difference between the valley of death and the Valley of the Shadow of Death? There is something which seems more deeply sinister about the Valley of the Shadow. There is the sense of impending danger, of threat. It is the war of nerves which life seems to be waging. The ax does not fall.

I do not see the ax but always there is squarely across my path, the Shadow of the Ax. Such extended experiences shatter the nerves and tend to demoralize the life. Fear of this quality seems completely destructive.

"I will fear no evil." When I *walk* through the *valley* of the *shadow* of death, I will fear no evil because God is with me. And His Presence makes the difference, because it cancels out the threatening element of the threat, the evil element of evil. Of course I may linger, or I may die; I may suffer acutely, or all my days may rest upon an undercurrent of muted agony. I shall not be overcome; God is with me. My awareness of God's Presence may sound like magic, it may seem to some to be the merest childlike superstition, but it meets my need and is at once the source of my comfort and the heart of my peace.

Though I walk through the Valley of the Shadow of Death,
I will fear no evil.


## 27. I Seek Room for Peace

I SEEK the enlargement of my heart that there may be room for Peace.

Already there is room enough for chaos. There is in every day's experience much that makes for confusion and bewilderment. Often I do not understand quite how my relations with others become frayed and chaotic. Sometimes this chaos is a positive thing; it means that something new, creative and whole is beginning to pull together the tattered fragments of my relationship with a person and to fashion it into that which delights the spirit and makes glad the heart. Sometimes the chaos is negative, a sign of degeneration in a relationship once meaningful and good. There is room enough for chaos.

But the need of my heart is for room for Peace: Peace of mind that inspires singleness of purpose; Peace of heart that quiets all fears and uproots all panic; Peace of spirit that filters through all confusions and robs them of their power. These I see NOW. I know that here in this quietness my life can be infused with Peace.

> Therefore, before God, I seek the enlargement of my
> heart at this moment, that there may be room for Peace.

## 28. Prayer for a Friendly World

OUR Father, fresh from the world, with the smell of life upon us, we make an act of prayer in the silence of this place. Our minds are troubled because the anxieties of our hearts are deep and searching. We are stifled by the odor of death which envelops our earth, where in so many places brother fights against brother. The panic of fear, the torture of insecurity, the ache of hunger, all have fed and rekindled ancient hatreds and long-forgotten memories of old struggles, when the world was young and Thy children were but dimly aware of Thy Presence in the midst. For all this, we seek forgiveness. There is no one of us without guilt and, before Thee, we confess our sins: we are proud and arrogant; we are selfish and greedy; we have harbored in our hearts and minds much that makes for bitterness, hatred and revenge.

While we wait in Thy Presence, search our spirits and grant to our minds the guidance and the wisdom that will teach us the way to take, without which there can be no peace and no confidence anywhere. Teach us how to put at the disposal of Thy Purposes of Peace the fruits of our industry, the products of our minds, the vast wealth of our land and the resources of our spirit. Grant unto us the courage to follow the illumination of this hour to the end that we shall not lead death to any man's door; but rather may we strengthen the hands of all in high places, and in common tasks seek to build a friendly world, of friendly men, beneath a friendly sky. This is the simple desire of our hearts which we share with Thee in thanksgiving and confidence.

## 29. Lord, Lord, Open Unto Me

Open unto me—light for
  my darkness.
Open unto me—courage for
  my fear.
Open unto me—hope for
  my despair.
Open unto me—peace for
  my turmoil.

Open unto me—joy for
  my sorrow.
Open unto me—strength for
  my weakness.
Open unto me—wisdom for
  my confusion.
Open unto me—forgiveness for
  my sins.
Open unto me—tenderness for
  my toughness.
Open unto me—love for
  my hates.
Open unto me—Thy Self for
  my self.

Lord, Lord, open unto me!

## 30. I Seek Truth and Light

I will keep my heart open to truth and light.

I WILL keep my heart open this day to all things that com-
mend themselves to me as truth. I will try to increase my
sensitiveness to error that it may not enter my heart with its
distortions and its falseness. This is not easy. I am never free
from the possibility of being mistaken. Deep within myself
I will be still, that I may be guided and wisened by the spirit
of God. In my own way, I will work out little tests by which
I may discern truth from error. Error may enter my mind and

heart in many disguises, this I know. My anxieties, my fears, my ambitions, even my hopes and my dreams may deceive me into calling truth, error; and error, truth. Always I will seek the honesty and integrity that God yields to those who lay bare their lives constantly before Him.

I will keep my heart open to light. There are times when the light burns, when it is too bright, or when it is too revealing. Somehow, I must accustom myself to the light and learn to look with steadiness at all that it discloses. I will not yield to the temptation to regard the light in me as being all the light there is. Always I will seek to let my steps be guided by such light as I have at any particular moment. Even in darkness I will learn to wait for the light, confident that it will come to cast its shaft across my path at the point of my greatest and most tragic need. Because God is the God of the darkness as well as the light, I shall be unafraid of the darkness.

I will keep my heart open to truth and light.


## 31. Be Thou my Vision

Be Thou my vision this day!

BE THOU my vision.

There are periods when all the margins of my awareness fade and I seem to be a wanderer lost in an unfamiliar land. Hard it is to focus, to make direction with my thoughts, my plans, my dreams. There are times when all clouds lift and before me looms, in brightest radiance, the goal so long sought. As I watch it and move more and more in the path which it describes before me, something happens. I do not know how—but the goal seems tawdry, less worthy than that which first sent me on my way. Now I seem more than lost—seem deserted, betrayed, not by the evil machinations of my mind, not by the willfulness of my own stubborn heart and mind—I seem betrayed by the vision, the goal itself. Be Thou my vision that I may have always before me, and within, the test, the checking point, of all my dreams; however whole, however glorious, however true they may seem to be.

Be Thou my vision this day.

I seek Thy vision not for tomorrow, not for some future day when I am more worthy and more prepared to know and understand. I seek Thy vision *this day*. Grant to me the flooding of my whole self with the light of Thy countenance that I may know directly when I have missed the way—when I have drifted out of the channel of Thy Purpose.

Be Thou my vision this day!

## 32. The Source of my Life

GOD is the source of all my life:

God is the source of my food:

Sometimes I forget that I am utterly dependent upon God for my food. When the farmer plants the seed, and when he cultivates the soil, the miracle of growth takes place. This miracle is an act of sheer grace; I do not cause it, I do not understand it, I cannot explain it—I can only describe it and that inadequately. It does not just happen. It is a part of an order, a way of behaving that is inherent in life itself. Truly, I am dependent upon God for my food.

The taste of food is not the result of my own effort. How wonderful is the miracle of taste! There is a mysterious inter-action between the tongue, my nervous system and the quality of food itself. How this developed, I do not know; what the secret is, always escapes me. The taste of food floats the whole eating experience and gives to it a dimension of delight that joys the mind and gives to the whole being a sense of gentleness and benevolence.

How can I say "Thank you" to God for food?

By making the eating of food a blessed sacrament.

By a self-conscious recognition of the source.

By SHARING my food with the hungry.

By knowing that my food is a gift of which I am merely the trustee.

Here in the quietness, I open my heart and mind to the need of others for food, which act is my salutation to God, the Source of all my life.

## 33. I Want to be Better

THE concern which I lay bare before God today is my need to be better:

I want to be better than I am in my most ordinary day-by-day contacts:
>With my friends—
>With my family—
>With my casual contacts—
>With my business relations—
>With my associates in work and play.

I want to be better than I am in the responsibilities that are mine:
>I am conscious of many petty resentments.
>I am conscious of increasing hostility toward certain people.
>I am conscious of the effort to be pleasing for effect, not because it is a genuine feeling on my part.
>I am conscious of a tendency to shift to other shoulders burdens that are clearly my own.

I want to be better in the quality of my religious experience:
>I want to develop an honest and clear prayer life.
>I want to develop a sensitiveness to the will of God in my own life.
>I want to develop a charitableness toward my fellows

that is far greater even than my most exaggerated
pretensions.
I want to be better than I am.

I lay bare this need and this desire before God in the quietness of this moment.


## 34.  I Need Courage

THE concern I lay bare before God today is my need for cour-
age:
I need courage to be honest—
Honest in my use of words
Honest in accepting responsibility
Honest in dealing with myself
Honest in dealing with my fellows
Honest in my relations with God

I need courage to face the problems of my own life—the
problems of personal values:
They are confused
They are often unreal
They are too exacting for comfort

The problems of my job:
Perhaps I am working at cross-purposes with my own
desires, ambitions, equipment.
Perhaps I am arrogant instead of taking pride in doing
work well.
Perhaps I am doing what I am doing just to prove a

point—spending a lifetime to prove a point that is
not worth proving after all.

Perhaps I have never found anything that could challenge me, and my life seems wasted.

Here in the quietness I lay bare before God my need for
courage, for the strength to be honest, for the guidance to
deal effectually with the problems of my own life.

O God, thou wilt not despise!

## 35. I Confess

THE concern which I lay bare before God today is:

My concern for the life of the world in these troubled times.
I confess my own inner confusion as I look out upon the
world.
There is food for all—many are hungry.
There are clothes enough for all—many are in rags.
There is room enough for all—many are crowded.
There are none who want war—preparations for con-
flict abound.

I confess my own share in the ills of the times.
I have shirked my own responsibilities as a citizen.
I have not been wise in casting my ballot.
I have left to others a real interest in making a public
opinion worthy of democracy.
I have been concerned about my own little job, my
own little security, my own shelter, my own bread.

I have not really cared about jobs for others, security
for others, shelter for others, bread for others.
I have not worked for peace; I want peace, but I have
voted
and worked for war.
I have silenced my own voice that it may not be heard
on the side of any cause, however right, if it meant
running risks or damaging my own little reputation.

Let Thy light burn in me that I may, from this moment on,
take effective steps within my own powers, to live up to
the light and courageously to pay for the kind of world I
so deeply desire.


## 36. Wrong Between Me and Thee

THE concern which I lay bare before God today is:

Whatever disaffection there is between me and those who
are or have been very close to me—
I seek the cause or root of such disaffection and, with the
illumination of the mind of God, to understand it.
I give myself to the scrutiny of God that, whatever there
may be in me that is responsible for what has happened,
I will acknowledge.
Where I have wronged or given offense deliberately or
without intention, I seek a face-to-face forgiveness.
Where I have been wronged or have taken offense delib-

erately or without intention, I seek a face-to-face forgiveness.

What I can undo I am willing to try; what I cannot undo, with that I seek to make my peace.

How to do these things, what techniques to use, with what spirit—for these I need and seek the wisdom and the strength of God.

Whatever disaffection there is between me and those who are or have been very close to me, I lay bare before God.

## 37. Not Comfortless

God will not leave me comfortless.

I FACE directly, squarely, the most stubborn facts of my present situation. I scrutinize each one of them as I list them in my mind:

One

Two

Three

Four

Five

This I have not done before. . . The result is a dimension of panic that I have never known. It is hard, so very hard, to hold my gaze steady—not to beat a retreat in pain, blame and self-recrimination. . .

Self-pity! ! !

Now something strange begins to happen. Long-forgotten words drift into the edges of my mind, weave in and out of the center of my concentration: "The Lord is my shepherd, I shall not want"; "I will lift up my eyes to the hills from whence cometh my help"; "Fear not, I am with you"; "The Lord is the strength of my life"; "Thy strength shall be as thy days."

My panic disintegrates and my insight into my own condition mounts until I see what I am to do and how! I can scarcely contain my joy—the wonder and the glory of my assurance—God has not left me comfortless.

God will not leave me comfortless.

## 38. I Rest This Day in God

I DO not seek the comfort of a guarantee that all my tomorrows will be safe and sure, that strength will be mine at a single time to carry all my need in the days ahead. This would be much, too much for such a one as I.
I rest this day in God.

I put in a single place all the pieces of my erring ways, the urgent thoughts both good and bad, together with my rights and wrongs. All in a single place they go. Here they lie where all is loss and all is gain, for they are mine. As for me—
I rest this day in God.

I do not seek to cast aside the burdens which are mine, to find
some easy way to lift the heavy load, to shift to other backs
what has found its way upon my own. They are mine, shaped
and fashioned in their own sure place—why? I am never sure.
But this I know—
I rest this day in God. . .

## 39. God Knows the Heart

God who knows the heart's secrets
Understands the Spirit's intention.

OFTEN we are reminded that the heart has secrets which it
cannot share with anyone, not even with itself. This is true
because there is in each one of us lingerings of desires that
have long since spent themselves in overt or direct action;
there are the throbs of impulses that have not become suf-
ficiently articulate to define themselves; there are vague reactions to experiences that are so much a part of our very
substance that we cannot distinguish them from our true
selves. And yet, all these and much more are a part of the
secrets of the heart.

The secrets of the heart are the raw material of the genuine
spirit of the individual. They are the stuff of the Spirit that
dwells deep within each one of us. When we pray, there is the
word that is spoken, the thought that is clearly defined, the
desire that is actively felt—and more! The "more" is the very

essence of the life's deep intent, it is the crucial units of shape-
less meanings that give to each life its quality and its flavor.

God knows the heart's secrets and deals with us at the level
of the heart's profoundest hunger. Where there is fear or
anxiety, these take precedence over the ebb and flow of the
inward tides. In order for the deepest things in us to be
touched and kindled, both fear and anxiety must be wiped
away. This we can do for ourselves, sometimes, but not often.
The one thing that they cannot abide is conscious exposure to
the Love of God.

> God who knows the heart's secrets
> Understands the Spirit's intention.

## 40. Courage to Live

*Give me courage to live—this day!*

I SEEK courage to live. It is not difficult to keep going—to
keep the flame of life burning—"as if to breathe were life."
The daily round may very easily be merely the daily round.
The common chores persist, going to bed and getting up, eating and making provisions for subsequent meals, talking day
by day the same talk, using the same set of well-worn con-
cepts, clichés and tired words. In one sense, it is good that this
is so. For it means that the mechanics of living can be learned
by heart and forgotten so that the resources of the personality
may be put completely at the disposal of the new way, the

fresh goal, the expanding horizon. I seek the courage to live.

I seek the courage to live—this day. How easily I slip into the mood that is desultory, that quietly informs my mind that tomorrow I can begin the new way, tomorrow I can make the fresh turning in my road. Courage to strike out on a path I have never trod before, courage to make new friends, courage to yield myself to the full power of the dream, courage to yield my life with abiding enthusiasm to the spirit of God and the wide reaches of His creative undertakings among the children of men— This I seek today.

Give me the courage to live—this day!

### 41. "I Will not Fail Thee"

> I will in no wise fail Thee
> Neither will I in any wise forsake Thee.

"I WILL in no wise fail Thee." There is always an insistent need for reassurance. Sometimes the need grows out of my own knowledge that the decision made is not a good decision. Often this discovery is made only after the crucial moment has passed and there seems to be nothing that I may do to make a change. Or it may come with great clarity at the very moment of decision, but all warning voices are ignored. Reassurance means in either instance that I shall pay, but not the full price, or that added strength will be mine to meet the full demand. It is no ordinary matter to foster a growing relationship with God that keeps watch over all the days and

the nights of all the years. "God will not fail me." I hold to
that in fair and stormy weather—I hold to it in the darkness
and in the light.

"Neither will I in any wise forsake Thee." This assurance
must not make me cautious or reckless. I must not abuse it
nor must I act stranger to it. It must not stretch me out of
shape so that I am stranger to myself, nor must it render me
immune to thoughtful procedures and to living with care. I
will make of this assurance the strong sure balance of my life.
I will embrace each new day with the enthusiasm of one who
is glad to be alive and shrinks from no challenge that con-
fronts me on my journey. I will not wait for guarantees other
than this when my best judgment says "yes." As I go to sleep
tonight and when I awake on tomorrow, I am comforted
immeasurably by the knowledge that

> God will in no wise fail me
> Neither will He in any wise forsake me.

## 42. God is Near to All

> God is near to all who call upon Him
> To all who call upon Him in truth.

GOD is near to all who call upon Him. Ofttimes I forget what
is the true source of my life. The urgencies of the daily
routine, the many anxieties that sweep over life like the tides
of the sea, the biting necessities which make so much of living
a ceaseless struggle, the private pains which make up the

great hurts in human experiences, the stifled hopes and gutted dreams that lie like bleached bones along the path—all these and much more put out of mind the solid assurance that nourishes life. This day must I remember that God is near—I shall call—and He will answer me.

God is near to all who call upon Him in truth. It is a naked, stripped feeling to act without one's customary pretensions. There is an intimate fear of being true—the fear of exposure, of being assaulted with no protecting shield. This fear carries over into the deep outreach of the heart. I call but do I truly expect an answer? Or am I fearful that there will be answer and I shrink from the responsibility that is implied? The call to God must be as genuine as my need; there must be the same radical earnestness of the reach for help as there is in the trepid agony of my need. This is to call upon God in truth. This I seek here and now to learn.

> God is near to all who call upon Him
> To all who call upon Him in truth.

## 43. The Fire Flower

THEY call it the fire flower—delicate pink as if it gathered unto its gentle petals the beauty of fading embers and dying flame. The story goes that its chief joy is to spring into life in the places that have been burned to blackened ash with nothing left to remind of grasses that were once green and shrubs that flourished in their own quaint or strident glory.

To spring into life with color and freshness where fire has burned and heat has laid waste—this is the quality and the grace of the fire flower.

I stood to gaze as the story was unfolded of the magic of this simple flower. Thought piled on thought until my mind seemed to choke with myriad currents rushing through the narrow channels of my little years. The thoughts brought each its image—sometimes a face long since unremembered —or an incident relived with joy or pain: The scene is a living room and the talk is gay and easy. Over in one corner, a voice mounts above the muted din of conversation—there is tenseness and then anger. Suddenly, all is silent—the silence of the sensed danger, the active threat. Eyes move stealthily in the same direction to reveal the speaker and the embarrassed countenance of his companion. Then a single voice, quiet and assured, moves into the vacuum with the word that heals and restores—the day was hot and the hill was long—I was tired and depressed. For hours I had wrestled with a very difficult examination for a permit to drive a car. I had failed utterly and my pride and spirit were crushed by the biting sarcasm of the examining officer. At the top of the hill I met a little boy—one of the dozens in the summer church school where I was working. Each day as a part of a simple worship, we repeated together: "And they helped each one his neighbor and everyone said to his comrade, Be of good cheer!" As soon as the little fellow saw me, he gave me a full-blown smile as he said, "Be of good cheer, Mr. Thurman."

Thus the images of the past came and went. Then there

were the faces of men and women who seem always to have the right word, the saving gesture, the simple deed that makes the barren place fruitful, the burned-over area to spring into life with color and freshness. What a gift of God, what a grace of life to be blessed with the magic of the fire flower!

## 44. Seek Ye the Lord

*Seek ye the Lord, while He may be found.*

SEEK ye the Lord. The impulse to align oneself on the side of that which is whole is a natural one. Sometimes it springs from the desire to cover up, to take refuge in the strength of another so as to shun the necessity of dealing with one's own weakness. Sometimes it springs from the desire to discover a way by which to understand one's own needs and to do something about meeting them. The Other-than-self reference is a necessity for peace of mind and spirit.

This day I seek the Lord. I seek to know God that I may understand myself, that I may grasp the true meaning of my own life and have its purpose increasingly defined. I seek His judgment that I may discern an ever clearer meaning between right and wrong courses of conduct. I seek His love that I may be inspired to love more and more what is good and true, and to transcend all barriers which stand between me and my fellows.

Seek ye the Lord while He is near. This does not mean that God will withdraw from me but it does mean that if I quench the desire to seek Him over and over again, there may come a time when the desire itself becomes buried beneath all kinds of debris in my own life. The desire will never die, but I must not run the risk of pushing it so far out of my consciousness that there seems to be no hunger in me to become whole, clean and redeemed.

Seek ye the Lord, while He may be found.

## 45. I Will Sing a New Song

THE old song of my spirit has wearied itself out. It has long ago been learned by heart so that now it repeats itself over and over, bringing no added joy to my days or lift to my spirit. It is a good song, measured to a rhythm to which I am bound by ties of habit and timidity of mind. The words belong to old experiences which once sprang fresh as water from a mountain crevice fed by melting snows. But my life has passed beyond to other levels where the old song is meaningless. I demand of the old song that it meet the need of present urgencies. Also, I know that the work of the old song, perfect in its place, is not for the new demand!

I will sing a new song. As difficult as it is, I must learn the new song that is capable of meeting the new need. I must fashion new words born of all the new growth of my life, my mind and my spirit. I must prepare for new melodies that have never been mine before, that all that is within me may lift my voice unto God. How I love the old familiarity of the wearied melody—how I shrink from the harsh discords of the new untried harmonies.

Teach me, my Father, that I might learn with the abandonment and enthusiasm of Jesus, the fresh new accent, the untried melody, to meet the need of the untried morrow. Thus, I may rejoice with each new day and delight my spirit in *each fresh* unfolding.

I will sing, this day, a new song unto Thee, O God.


## 46. The Wisdom of God

The Wisdom of God is my abiding strength.

KNOWLEDGE abounds on every hand by which my steps may be guided. Facts, facts, facts . . . they are everywhere about me. I know with my mind the meaning of many choices that I make. Besides there are many sources upon which I may draw for information that will be the raw material of my decisions. But facts are not the heart of my need.

I need wisdom. The quality that will make clear to me the significance, the relatedness of things that are a part of my daily experience—this I lack again and again. I need wisdom to cast a slow and steady radiance over all my landscape in order that things, choices, deeds may be seen in their true light—the light of the eternal and the timeless.

The wisdom of God—how can I abide without it? If that

ⁱis withdrawn then I am forced to lean on my own understanding or the understanding and opinions of others. The wisdom of God can flood even the error of my ways and transform my error into a path of light. He has been at work in life longer than my days and the days of man's long journey and will give to me the full sweep of His spirit even in my little life and its big problems. This I know. Therefore:

The Wisdom of God is my abiding strength.


## 47. Give Me the Listening Ear

Give me the listening ear
The eye that is willing to see.

GIVE me the listening ear. I seek this day the ear that will not shrink from the word that corrects and admonishes—the word that holds up before me the image of myself that causes me to pause and reconsider—the word that challenges me to deeper consecration and higher resolve—the word that lays bare needs that make my own days uneasy, that seizes upon every good decent impulse of my nature, channeling it into paths of healing in the lives of others.

Give me the listening ear. I seek this day the disciplined mind, the disciplined heart, the disciplined life that makes my ear the focus of attention through which I may become mindful of expressions of life foreign to my own. I seek the stimulation that lifts me out of old ruts and established habits which keep me conscious of my self, my needs, my personal interests.

Give me this day—the eye that is willing to see the meaning of the ordinary, the familiar, the commonplace—the eye that is willing to see my own faults for what they are—the eye that is willing to see the likable qualities in those I may not like—the mistake in what I thought was correct—the strength in what I had labeled as weakness. Give me the eye that is willing to see that Thou hast not left Thyself without a witness in every living thing. Thus to walk with reverence and sensitiveness through all the days of my life.

> Give me the listening ear
> The eye that is willing to see.

## 48. The Moments of High Resolve

> Keep fresh before me
> The moments of my high resolve.

DESPITE the dullness and barrenness of the days that pass, if I search with due diligence, I can always find a deposit left by some former radiance. But I had forgotten. At the time it was full-orbed, glorious and resplendent. I was sure that I would never forget. In the moment of its fullness, I was sure that it would illumine my path for all the rest of my journey I had forgotten how easy it is to forget.

There was no intent to betray what seemed so sure at the

time. My response was whole, clean, authentic. But little by little, there crept into my life the dust and grit of the journey. Details, lower-level demands, all kinds of crosscurrents— nothing momentous, nothing overwhelming, nothing flagrant —just wear and tear. If there had been some direct challenge —a clear-cut issue—I would have fought it to the end, and beyond.

In the quietness of this place, surrounded by the all-pervading Presence of God, my heart whispers: Keep fresh before me the moments of my High Resolve, that in fair weather or in foul, in good times or in tempests, in the days when the darkness and the foe are nameless or familiar, I may not forget that to which my life is committed.

> Keep fresh before me
> The moments of my high resolve.

## 49. Surrounded by the Love of God

*I am surrounded by the love of God.*

THE earth beneath my feet is the great womb out of which the life upon which my body depends comes in utter abundance. There is at work in the soil a mystery by which the death of one seed is reborn a thousandfold in newness of life. The magic of wind, sun and rain creates a climate that nourishes every living thing. It is law, and more than law; it is order, and more than order—there is a brooding tenderness out of which it all comes. In the contemplation of the earth, I know that I am surrounded by the love of God.

The events of my days strike a full balance of what seems both good and bad. Whatever may be the tensions and the stresses of a particular day, there is always lurking close at hand the trailing beauty of forgotten joy or unremembered peace. The weakness that engulfs me in its writhing toils reveals hidden strengths that could not show their face until my own desperation called them forth. In the contemplation of the events of my days, I know that I am surrounded by the love of God.

The edge of hope that constantly invades the seasoned grounds of despair, the faith that keeps watch at the doors through which pass all the labors of my life and heart for what is right and true, the impulse to forgive and to seek forgiveness even when the injury is sharp and clear—these and countless other things make me know that by day and by night my life is surrounded by the love of God.

I am surrounded by the love of God.

## 50. For a Time of Sorrow

I share with you the agony of your grief,
    The anguish of your heart finds echo in my own.
    I know I cannot enter all you feel
    Nor bear with you the burden of your pain;
I can but offer what my love does give:
    The strength of caring,

The warmth of one who seeks to understand
The silent storm-swept barrenness of so great a loss.
This I do in quiet ways,
That on your lonely path
You may not walk alone.

## 51. Against Thee have I Sinned

Against Thee have I sinned
O Lord, forgive!

THE recollection of wrongdoing is vivid before me, this day. It is not hard to recognize wrongdoing when it takes its toll in the lives of those around me. The little deed of meanness in which some grudge is satisfied seems to be registered only against the person for whom it is intended. Deeper meditation brings before me in radical manifestation the awful truth that it is against God that the meanness is done. I shrink from the bald fact—I cover up with many explanations, neat ideas and clever notions. In the moment of prayer all of these vanish and what is left? The steady awareness that the wrongdoing has an ultimate meaning, it is against the Highest thing in me, the Highest thing in life, that I have sinned. It is against God.

I seek forgiveness. It is wonderful to be forgiven by the person, and often this seems to be sufficient. But deep within, I know that this is not the end of the matter. It is merely the beginning. Somehow, I must become reconciled with the

Highest thing in me, the Highest thing in life. I must become reconciled with God. This I discover almost like a flash of blinding light when I pray. Here at last, I know that it is always against God that evil is done. It is then that with all my heart I say:

> Against Thee have I sinned
> O Lord, forgive!

## 52. Teach Me Thy Will

SOMETIMES I am conscious that my actions flow from the will or the wills of others. It may be because I am trying very hard to please others even at the cost of what may be very precious deep within me. Subtle indeed is the temptation to be pleasing in the sight of others; to be "all things to all men" is the phrase the apostle uses. This desire to be pleasing is both disturbing and rewarding.

Sometimes I am conscious that my actions flow from a will that is my own. There are decisions that are my decisions and mine alone. Again and again, such decisions may not arise out of my own sense of values or even of truth but may spring from the intensity of my own desire or my own need. But when I am more myself and I look upon my actions, something in me denies the integrity of the thing I have done. This does not happen with great frequency but when it does, the night is very dark indeed.

Teach me Thy will. Teach me to dig deep enough within me to strike the mainspring of Thy life that flows through me that I may discover Thy Will for my daily living even as for my life. I seek Thy Will in order that I may be whole in my inward parts and that there may be no conflict between the good I see and the good I am... Thus no conflict between my inner and my outer.

Teach me Thy will, O God!

## 53. God Restoreth my Soul

THE ravages of time are at work in me. I remember when to do the wrong thing brought sharp and swift judgment to my mind and to my spirit. Then there followed a period when much in me that was sensitive to error grew dull and numb. There was no marked and dramatic change—simply the quiet wearing away of the sharp and pointed consciousness of wrong. Until, at last, there were the dead places, the barren spots. It may have been some passing remark from a thoughtful friend, or a flash of light from a forgotten moment of searching prayer, or a challenge to sympathy to which my mind alone responded but of which my feelings were unaware. Then I knew how far I had drifted, and in the wake of that awareness God moved with the swiftness of the eagle in the hunt. The miracle had happened—He had restored my soul.

The drain on my spirit from so much of hardship, the tearing of the brambles in my path, have taken their toll. All the energies seem to spend themselves merely in keeping going. The excuses of weariness and exhaustion seemed ever at hand and anxious to serve. Again and again, the words flowed into me—It takes too much effort to go the second mile—Why should I care so much, no one else seems to be bothered—It is all I can do to handle the necessities of my own life and that I do poorly . . . on and on the stream flowed unchecked. Then, somewhere along the way, all seemed wrong. I took time aside for checking before God. I told Him all about my increasing dullness, wearisome detail after wearisome detail. When I finished, I was spent. While I waited in my exhaustion, Strength and Renewal were at work in me. Weakness made strong—exhaustion transformed into energies. Deep within there was born the declaration that this risk I must not ever run again. I know now that God restoreth the soul moment by moment, if the door is not held tightly against Him or if it is not permitted to jam by too much of cares and weariness.

God restoreth my soul!

## 54. If Thou Standeth Beside Me

If Thou standeth beside me<br>Nothing can prevail against me.

"IF THOU standeth beside me." There are times when the sense of aloneness is very acute. Often these are times of struggle where the odds are uneven. Curious indeed is it that the sense of not being alone is apt to be most acutely felt when the concentration upon the matter at hand is absorbing. This means that there is available, at the moment, no margin of me exposed to the Presence of God. To be aware that God is standing beside me calls for some measure of detachment from my own personal struggle and turmoil.

"If Thou standeth beside me." It is entirely possible that the Presence of God may be most acutely felt in and through the struggle and the turmoil. It is not something apart from my involvements but a quality of Presence that emerges from the midst of my tempests. Or more accurately, it becomes a quality of the tempest itself. Sometimes this identification becomes very confusing, causing me to say that God brings the struggle. It is sufficient for me to know that He is found in the midst of all that befalls me. Nothing can prevail against me. The affirmation is the result of the disclosure of the Presence of God in the midst of what befalls me. First, He is felt as being with, in and among the struggling elements of my experience. Then, out of the midst of these, His Presence emerges and becomes One who stands by my side. It is then that I am lifted up and strengthened.

> If Thou standeth beside me
> Nothing can prevail against me.